OUTSMART
YOUR
INSTINCTS

How The Behavioral Innovation™ Approach
Drives Your Company Forward

Adam Hansen, Edward Harrington, and Beth Storz

Published by Forness Press™
Minneapolis, MN
www.ideastogo.com

Distributed by Greenleaf Book Group

For ordering information or special discounts for bulk purchases, please contact Greenleaf Book Group at PO Box 91869, Austin, TX 78709, 512.891.6100.

Design and composition by Greenleaf Book Group and Kim Lance
Cover design by Greenleaf Book Group and Kim Lance
Cover images: © iStock Collection / rashadashurov; © iStock Collection / fireflamenco; © iStock Collection / GoMixer

Cataloging-in-Publication data is available.

Print ISBN: 978-0-9973845-0-5

eBook ISBN: 978-0-9973845-1-2

Part of the Tree Neutral® program, which offsets the number of trees consumed in the production and printing of this book by taking proactive steps, such as planting trees in direct proportion to the number of trees used: www.treeneutral.com

TreeNeutral®

Printed in the United States of America on acid-free paper

16 17 18 19 20 21   10 9 8 7 6 5 4 3 2 1

First Edition

Contents

Foreword   vii

1: Introduction   1

2: Negativity Bias—Bad Is Stronger than Good   15

3: Availability Bias—What You See Is All There Is   45

4: The Curse of Knowledge—Well, It's Just Obvious that . . .   69

5: Status Quo Bias—The Bird in the Hand   85

6: Confabulation—Of Course That's Why I Did That!   105

7: Conformity Bias—Play Along to Get Along   125

8: Confirmation Bias—Just As I Thought!   143

9: Framing—Like a Fish in Water   163

10: Steps Forward   189

11: Conclusion   201

Acknowledgments   205

Notes   209

Self-Assessment and Activity Guide   215

Index   229

About the Authors   236

Foreword

I WAS BORN IN MINNESOTA IN 1928, THE YEAR THAT ALSO GAVE BIRTH to the best-known innovation of the 20th century—sliced bread. No one actually acknowledged it as an "innovation" back then, because the word wasn't yet a familiar term. But now that the concept is widespread and here to stay, I see *innovation* as an ideal label for what we have always done at Ideas To Go: help people think outside the box and outsmart their instincts so they can create something new that will be of use to others. And, we utilize our own processes internally to keep advancing the services we provide.

What really drives me is my interest in how people work together— or don't, in many cases. Early on in my career in brand management and advertising—first with Procter & Gamble, then with Campbell Mithun—I found that "people problems" were a constant drain on everyone's energy, including my own. As my career progressed, I wanted to figure out how to get people to think more openly—and work more effectively, efficiently, *and creatively* together. But it wasn't until I discovered George Prince's work in creative meeting dynamics and got hooked on the Osborn-Parnes Creative Problem Solving model, that I began to envision a process to create real change in the way we think about innovating.

I started using these new tools to facilitate sessions for clients who were seeking new product ideas and looking to evolve their brand's personalities and communication. Suddenly, what used to take three to four months of discussion and development was now happening in three to four weeks. More important, my clients loved it. I got a huge kick out of people going home from those sessions on a high. They said they had an easier time seeing what was *good*, and finding more possibilities to go "for" in life—not just at work, but at home, too. Hearing that from clients was a big *Aha!* for me. And, as often happens with big ahas, I felt compelled to leave my agency job and create my own thing. That was the spark that ignited Ideas To Go (ITG).

As I said before, innovation as a concept was just getting off the ground. But I began to see collaborative innovation as the intersection between inspiring people's inherent creative abilities and fostering their willingness to work together. And we all had to agree, at the very least, not to kill a new idea—and, at our very best, to open up our thinking to consider all sorts of wonderful nonsense and "out there" possibilities in the pursuit of breakthrough ideas.

I see in hindsight, understanding the *Behavioral Innovation*™ approach (BI) is an important tool to getting the larger innovation equation right. BI exposes the cognitive biases that block creative thinking and under-mine innovation—and harnesses them to propel innovation forward.

For me, the clearest obstacle to innovation and the most deeply entrenched bias is the Negativity Bias mindset. This is our natural instinct to play it safe and kill new ideas—allowing us to appear to be a criti-cal thinker and, therefore, smart. To combat this, I concocted *Forness*® thinking—Ideas To Go's not-so-secret weapon against Negativity Bias. I came up with the term while flying to a client project in Maryland. I needed a headline, a simple way to get my clients to buy into the creative problem-solving process—and keep it positive. If there is anything that is important in the innovation process, it is working hand in hand with the people who need your output. So I decided to ask my clients to focus on what they were FOR in an idea, as opposed to what they were against.

I then asked them what they still WISHED FOR in this idea, as a way of pushing towards solutions—instead of just listing problems, obstacles, and concerns. The idea worked. *Forness®* thinking, enforced by a strict "No, Yes But" rule, still drives the Ideas To Go process today.

As I mentioned earlier, I was born quite some time ago. If my life has been dedicated to anything, it has been to helping people find ways to get past conflict and get along. And that's not pie in the sky. A well-structured process can propel people toward new opportunities, without them feeling threatened. I got into this business because I like working with nice people who have imaginations, are fairly bright, treat each other well, and are just fun to be around. That's the definition of the folks at ITG. I also like working in that same manner with a client group—and once they really get turned on to *Forness®* thinking and our process—they seem to like it too. And that feels especially good to me.

I'm proud of what we've created at Ideas To Go, and so pleased that ITG continues to practice what we preach—innovating from within and breaking ground in new territory like the *Behavioral Innovation™* approach. My granddaughter now works as an Innovation Process Facilitator at ITG (as did her mother before her!) and she just told me they have a new mobile app that helps people use *Forness®* thinking and ideate on the go. I started living mostly "off the grid" when I left my computer at ITG around 2001—but when I hear about something like that mobile app, my mind immediately goes to, *Oh my god! The things we could be doing with that!* I can't wait to see what the ITG gang will think of next.

Fred Meyer
Founder, Ideas To Go

1

Introduction

YOUR GREAT-GREAT-GREAT-GREAT-GREAT-GREAT- (YOU GET THE POINT) grandfather and his friend are out walking in the jungle one bright, fine day. They hear a rustling in the bushes. The friend goes out to investigate. He finds himself cornered by a tiger and—pardon the horror—meets his demise as a delicious side of man-kabobs for the hungry predator. Your ancestor runs the other direction, and so lives to see another day. His takeaway? What you can't see might kill you. So it's safe to assume the unknown might just be another tiger looking for a meal. Bottom line: stay away from the unknown.

Fast-forward a few hundred generations. The same kind of reaction toward the unknown occurs again and again—those who take quick, decisive action to avoid novelty are more likely to have stuck around long enough to pass on their DNA. We are the descendants of the savants of risk aversion. We come by this impulse honestly. Our bodies and minds are still structured for the needs of millennia past; and just as the real threat to our bodies now isn't caloric scarcity, but caloric overabundance (despite having bodies still wired to avoid caloric scarcity), our minds are also still wired to avoid existential threats and other now-rare problems. Many of our instincts are still prepared to deal with a reality that no longer exists.

We learn from the field of Behavioral Decision Making, which draws on Psychology and Behavioral Economics, that this is just one of the many Cognitive Biases humans have developed—Negativity Bias. Cognitive Biases are a collection of mental shortcuts that have evolved in our brains over time, shaping our judgment of the world. And social scientists confirm that all humans have them—across age groups, across cultures. To be human is to have Cognitive Biases.

Although they were once a useful tool to keep us safe from threats (like hungry tigers) and aid in quick decision making—all important when survival was what most aspired to—when it comes to the world of innovation, Negativity Bias and other Cognitive Biases can stymie even the most adept thinkers. You've seen it time and time again. A manager who's afraid to try a new product development process because it's just too unproven. Or a researcher who discounts suspect data—nonconsciously—to confirm what he thinks he already knows. Or a group of like-minded colleagues who are eager to enact real change, but still encounter roadblocks, often within themselves, without entirely understanding why.

Cognitive Biases make innovation difficult. From the momentum-killing lead shoes of Negativity Bias to the limiting blinders of Availability Bias; from the "stay-in-bounds" electric fence of Conformity Bias to the revisionist history we get from the Curse of Knowledge, we see these biases every day, unnecessarily making the challenge of innovation trickier. And we're far from immune—we see it in ourselves daily.

But we have a secret. With the right tools and techniques it's possible to transform biases from roadblocks that hinder innovation into exciting opportunities to think differently. We believe that with aware-ness of these Cognitive Biases, we can not only overcome them, but increase our understanding of all the people involved in the effort to go from concept to market—our customers, our partners, and ourselves.

It's why we were compelled to write this book. We think the best place to start is awareness. So let's start at the beginning and focus on the star of this show: your brain.

System 1 and System 2 Thinking

Your brain is one of the hardest-working organs in your body, consum-ing about 20 percent of your energy while representing only 2 percent of your body mass. As such, your brain has developed ingenious ways to conserve energy—powering up and down its processing power based upon the demands of each task.

In his book *Thinking, Fast and Slow*, Daniel Kahneman describes how our brains have two distinct modes of thinking to help us make the most of our resources.

System 1 (**Fast**) is the "easy" type of thinking that our mind defaults to unless there's a compelling reason to take on harder thinking. It's also referred to as intuitive thinking. It's nonconscious and automatic. It takes almost no effort for System 1 thinking to kick in and direct the show, so it's also pretty energy-efficient. Behind this efficiency is a very sophisticated pattern-recognition system. It seems simple to us because lots of hard work has already been devoted to programing System 1 for "automatic pilot" by dealing with complex subtleties and inferring con-sistencies, all outside our awareness. For example, you might remem-ber how much attention and concentration it took to learn how to drive when you were a teenager. You had to pay attention to the hundreds of details such as the sides of the road, the car ahead of you, the car behind you (that you saw in that little rearview mirror in front of you), and when it was time to put on the blinker before you made a left-hand turn at a busy intersection. After many years on the road, the process has become automatic, and we don't always know when to switch back from "automatic pilot" to more careful attention.

In the same manner, our brains shift most of our habitual decision-making to automatic pilot, and for many daily tasks and decisions, System 1 thinking does most of the work—the heavy lifting. You have undoubtedly driven all the way home from work without any conscious memory of going through the motions of driving the car. The same process takes place when we decide what we like and don't like, or what we think will work and what won't work. We don't take the time to evaluate every variable and look for new or subtle sources of information. We react automatically and direct our own behavior accordingly. We couldn't get through the day without the efficiencies of System 1.

One of the places we see System 1 thinking most frequently in our business is during the idea-generation phase. This phase is usually fast paced and lots of fun. Our brains are making lots of nonconscious and intuitive connections. As facilitators, we're often directing participants in drawing pictures and playing games to stimulate new thinking and get past the habitual, logical, and limited. For most people, it's an engaging and enjoyable process.

But, the System 1 thinking that makes all that efficiency possible is also home to our nonconscious Cognitive Biases. These mental shortcuts are *always* influencing our thinking, and potentially hindering our range of ideas, even when it feels like ideas are flowing freely.

For example, these Cognitive Biases often influence our decision making when it's time to choose which ideas to move forward. Because a large share of processing happens outside of awareness, we can be blind to the cognitive errors that ensue. And to make matters worse, System 1 can also lead us to be unjustifiably confident—like Steve Carell's character, Michael Scott, in the US version of *The Office*—so when we rely solely on this intuitive thinking, we can make errors and omissions, often unknowingly. It's like the old adage, "It is when you think you are the most right that you are at risk of being the most wrong." Anyone who has ever been married can vouch for this assertion. We need to be aware of our various System 1 instincts that both make our life easier *and* can trip us up at important moments.

System 2 (**Slow**) is thinking that requires more effort, more focus, and more conscious thought. It's often called conscious thinking, or reflective thinking. It's the more deliberate and deliberative part of our thinking process. Think of Rodin's statue "The Thinker." A hard cognitive task just might require us to sit down and ruminate for a bit, perhaps with our chin resting on our hand. System 2 requires a lot more energy. To conserve our mental "bandwidth," our brains don't like to be bothered unnecessarily if System 1 thinking can handle the task. While both modes of thinking are happening all the time, System 2 is generally relegated to monitoring and ratifying the decisions of System 1. System 2 is only activated in response to particular circumstances—like when the stakes are high, when an obvious error is detected, or when careful reasoning is required.

Robust innovation and creative problem-solving processes require some serious System 2 thinking. While there's plenty of System 1 thinking involved along the way, if you neglect System 2 thinking when it's needed, you will miss out on some really good ideas; you might even make some bad judgment calls that could have been avoided if you had engaged System 2 more.

We frequently see our clients trying to avoid engaging in System 2 thinking immediately after Idea Generation, when it's time to select which ideas will move forward. That's the time when we have to take a deliberate look at all the great ideas we have generated and narrow them down to a manageable set to move forward. Suddenly, it all becomes . . . A lot. Less. Fun.

At this point, it's pretty typical for teams to start avoiding System 2 thinking (even though they're not consciously aware of their resistance), and it's our job as Facilitators to counter the objections and ensure that the needed deliberate thinking will happen. The objections will be couched in seemingly rational arguments. For example, people will say, "It takes too long to review all the ideas. We don't have time," or "Let's just have everyone champion a few ideas instead of reviewing all of them. The ones we remember are probably the best ones anyway." But don't be fooled by these clever excuses. It's merely a group of brains trying to conserve energy.

But to be clear, System 1 thinking isn't just random associations. There are some real benefits that can be used to our advantage for fast decisions when the stakes aren't too high:

- System 1 works well when the choice between Option A and Option B simply isn't a big deal or is a habitual choice. Think about different brands of pasta sauce, or weekend video-on-demand options. These choices aren't ones you're going to take too much time on . . . unless you're a really discriminating marinara connoisseur or have a deep-seated love for John Cusack movies.

- System 1 is especially helpful when we have developed enough expertise in a given area that we can rely on our well-honed powers of pattern recognition to guide us quickly without having to think very hard. This is actually the brilliant observation behind Malcolm Gladwell's best-selling book *Blink*. Experts have ways of knowing (System 1) that they can't even explain (with System 2). Gladwell points out that an experienced art appraiser can spot a forgery but may not be able to say exactly what's wrong with the piece. You and I will also have our "gut reactions," but we wouldn't want to spend a lot of money without consulting an expert, who has trained intuitions from facing certain decisions so many times that the patterns become automatic.

Bounded Rationality

A slightly different take on this process is the concept of *Bounded Rationality*. Classical economics has at its root the idea of the Rational Actor, who is assumed to have:

1. Unlimited time.

2. Unfettered access to information.

Under these mythical conditions, the hypothetical "Rational Actor" will always make the most logical and value-maximizing decisions that are always in their own best interests. And while computers can do the calculations to determine how the "Rational Actor" would behave, real people never make decisions that way. The fact is, time and access to information are *always* limited—or at least bounded by practical constraints and daily pressures. Herbert Simon, who first proposed this concept, suggests that we more often use rules of thumb, or "heuristics," rather than rigid rules of optimization, because we have other important decisions to make elsewhere, and our brains aren't designed to make these kinds of calculations at all. Life is short. The modern trend of "so much to do, so little time," requires more and more efficiency and multitasking. Luckily, a lot of our decisions don't really require much attention, so it's often adaptive to make use of our own heuristics. And they serve us pretty well—as long as we don't mind "thinking inside the box."

Behavioral Economics Moves Forward

We've recently seen the key insights from Behavioral Economics (BE) move into other fields of human endeavor, such as Behavioral Ethics, Behavioral Law, and Behavioral Health Policy. One of the lead BE researchers, Professor Cass Sunstein, even served as the Administrator of the Office of Information and Regulatory Affairs in the Obama administration. One of his primary contributions was to incorporate key BE insights in communicating and incentivizing regulatory compliance, and this approach has also been embraced by British Prime Minister David Cameron's team. BE principles transcend political parties, as they speak to what it really means to be human, on both sides of the aisle.

In a field that is so dependent on applying a better understanding of human behavior, it's time for Innovation to embrace *Behavioral Innovation*™. We know by now that we are all "predictably irrational" (as Dan Ariely observed)—hardly the Rational Actor that was proposed by Simon in the 1970s. Through the lens of Behavioral Innovation, many conundrums that "innovationistas" have wrestled with for decades are becoming more understandable. We now know better than ever how to recognize and overcome some of the more vexing obstacles in our own cognition, and facilitate more creative thinking in the stakeholders we serve—including customers, channel partners, and regulators.

The Cognitive Biases of Innovation

So, now that we know we are fighting against our own prehistoric cognitive wiring, what can we do? We need to work constantly and consciously on compensating for these "bugs" in our cognition to reduce their innovation-inhibiting forces. The first step is to recognize the role of specific Cognitive Biases when they are operating nonconsciously in System 1 so we can strategically call upon System 2 to take us to another level of innovation. While it's helpful to be aware of the longer list of Cognitive Biases, there are eight biases that we see impeding innovation on a regular basis, including:

- **Negativity Bias**: "Bad is stronger than good." Since the Cognitive Biases were developed to keep us safe from perceived threats, "bad" is always more salient than good. We fear loss more than we appreciate gain. As such, negativity has a more powerful effect on our thinking and behavior than positivity does. Metaphor: lead shoes unnecessarily slowing you down when you're trying to move forward.

- **Availability Bias:** "What you see is all there is." When making decisions, we tend to go straight to what we can recall most quickly and easily, and often miss things—such as valuable information and a more realistic sense of likely outcomes—that could lead to better decisions. More vivid memories (including more negative ones) will stand out and skew our judgment. Metaphor: horse blinders focusing you only on what's right in front of you.

- **Curse of Knowledge:** "Well, it's just obvious that . . ." Once we become experts in something, we have a hard time placing ourselves back into a position of someone who lacks that knowledge, no matter how much we believe we can. We assume that others have waaay too much prior knowledge and have trouble taking their perspective and explaining our ideas in a way that they understand. As difficult as it can be to know something, it is also difficult to "unknow" it. Metaphor: revisionist history that comes to be accepted as conventional wisdom, but isn't quite the whole story.

- **Status Quo Bias:** "The bird in the hand." In every proposed course of action, the automatic default/safest position is to keep things as they are and to ratify previous decisions. We believe that we can't be criticized for making a bad decision if we merely endorse the Status Quo—incumbency gives it power that it often doesn't deserve. Metaphor: balloon ballast keeping you from getting very far off the well-trodden ground.

- **Confabulation:** "Of course that's why I did that!" We often make decisions emotionally—and not as systematically as we believe—and then pull together plausible-enough justification for these decisions. We usually believe that our manufactured rationale is true. We're not lying, we're just not fully aware of why we chose what we chose. And besides, it sounds so plausible. Metaphor: unreliable eyewitnesses who believe fervently they saw what they say, but in reality saw only a fraction of what happened, and even that was influenced by the emotion of the moment.

- **Conformity Bias:** "Play along to get along." This is the need for agreement in a group that keeps us from exploring alternative perspectives. By putting more focus on agreement than on the quality of the decision itself, we end up making worse decisions. Metaphor: a pet's "electric fence" collar keeping us well within the safest boundaries, usually to excess.

- **Confirmation Bias:** "Just as I thought." This is the tendency to seek out evidence that supports the position we've already embraced regardless of whether the information is true—and ignore anything that contradicts our preconceived notion. We subconsciously skew how new evidence is evaluated depending on its support of our previous decisions. Metaphor: the royal courtiers in the "Emperor's New Clothes" who strain to maintain the agreed-upon reality.

- **Framing:** "Like a fish in water." This is how individuals, groups, and societies organize, perceive, and communicate about reality. Our frame is the mental picture we have of our world; it's the paradigm through which we perceive reality. It encompasses our nonconscious assumptions that help us make daily decisions. We often don't even think of the frame when ideas are served up to us. Metaphor: the official tour of a totalitarian state given to visiting foreign heads of state. What you *do* see is probably true, albeit polished to its shiniest. It's what you *don't* see that's distorting your take on what's really going on.

So imagine this extra cast of characters and props accompanying you throughout your day. Going into every meeting with you. Crowding into your office or cubicle even when you're working alone. Squeezing into the meeting room even when you're coming together to do your best, most creative, most meaningful work. It's not just the elephant in the room that we need to acknowledge—it's these eight additional influences, demanding their due. And we can't do anything about them if we don't remind ourselves they're there with us. These particular instincts of ours make innovation unnecessarily challenging.

Let's get to work!

Chapter Structure

We will examine each of these Cognitive Biases through the first three stages of Innovation, commonly referred to as "the Funnel" or as seen in a Stage-Gate process in New Product Development: Opportunity Identification, Ideation, and Concept Development.

1. **Opportunity Identification (Opportunity ID).** This is the stage of determining where we're going to play. This is one of the first big opportunities to innovate—if you define your big innovation opportunity areas "innovatively" and differently than the rest of the category does, you're already a step ahead for innovation. Often big Benefit Areas or Need States, these opportunity areas are not the innovation possibilities themselves. This should be a very creative endeavor, not just an exercise of checking the boxes of category assumption. Your company/brand should have a different point of view (POV) on this vital starting point than the rest of the field has. Great framing of your biggest opportunities gets momentum going toward breakthrough possibilities within them. To illustrate, if we were getting ready to play with Legos, this would be deciding where we would focus on a broad level; for example, today is about building castles, not racecars, and landing on eight to ten different categories of castles that we were going to play with.

2. **Ideation.** This stage involves moving the big opportunity areas forward, and fleshing them out with specific possibilities to start to see what all you can do within those areas. Ideation is the classic image of creativity in innovation. Ideation is about generating 10 to 100 times more ideas than you first think you need in order to open up fresh space you couldn't have anticipated in advance, solving for Uniqueness first, then adding in more Relevance to

increase your odds of hitting the sweet spot. Ideation should tap into the realities of the customer's lived experience and should be contextual—we're not generating possibilities in a vacuum. Creating fodder for the Who, What, When, Where, Why, and How will give you lots of great building blocks for Concept Development. Lego metaphor here: let's get hundreds of different, cool pieces and groups of pieces together to create lots of different castles later across the eight to ten different castle types.

3. **Concept Development.** This stage is about synthesis of the great output from Ideation, not necessarily direct extraction. It's about pulling together different "mini-stories" that bring possibilities to life—assembling at least a few of the Who/What/Why/etc. questions. It's still about pushing Uniqueness and new forms of Relevance, so we don't immediately trade away all the energy from Ideation for the sake of practicality and Launch readiness. Usually the next big milestone is about Learning (not Launch), and so we should design concepts to maximize the Learning opportunity. The Lego metaphor here is building a dozen distinct types of castles, from those closer in to the expected template to some further out and pleasantly surprising.

While the "center of gravity" for a given Cognitive Bias might be more pronounced in one of these three stages, we have found that it is critically important to be vigilant for all eight biases in each of these stages. Even the act of taking a moment to see if a Cognitive Bias might be operating will help you win the battle within.

So why is it so hard to do innovation right?

It's because some of our ways of viewing the world, though they've worked well over the past millennia, will trip us up if we're not conscious of them and don't take specific steps to mitigate their downsides as we move forward. It's because the deck is stacked against us—we don't start at zero, but carry instinctual baggage that doesn't serve us well. It's because the enemy is within our own brains—and we, ourselves, are killing innovation.

2

Negativity Bias—Bad Is Stronger than Good

*"Whatever it is, I'm against it. No matter what it is or who
commenced it, I'm against it! Your proposition may be good but let's
have one thing understood, whatever it is, I'm against it!
And even when you've changed it or condensed it, I'm against it!"*

—*Horse Feathers*, Groucho Marx (1933)

IT'S BEEN PROVEN THAT NEGATIVE INFORMATION, EXPERIENCES, AND
even negative people have a stronger effect on us than positive ones. As
Baumeister et al. argued in their 2001 academic article, "Bad Is Stronger
than Good":[1]

- Negative emotions and authority figures have more impact than
  good ones.

- Negative information is retained better in our memory than positive info.

- Negative impressions form more quickly and are tougher to counter than good ones.

All told, the research findings show that bad is stronger than good, both as a general principle and also across a broad range of psychological phenomena. Other research shows that critics who provide negative evaluations are seen as more intelligent than positive evaluators, even when the content of their evaluations is of equal quality.[2]

This phenomenon is called the Negativity Bias, and it sits at the gnarled root of many of the Cognitive Biases that make it so hard to do innovation right. As Daniel Kahneman observed, we are simply hardwired to "treat threats as more urgent than opportunities." Historically, this mindset increased our odds of surviving to the next day, and with enough "next days" we eventually pass on our DNA and shape the gene pool of humanity accordingly. Stated differently, we are all the descendants of loss-aversion savants—because those less adept at mitigating risks were less likely to win the genetic contest of "survival of the fittest." Those who took quick, decisive action in the face of even a whiff of negative uncertainty were more likely to thrive, while those who paused to consider all the possibilities in threatening situations were less likely to survive when the major downside risk was an untimely death. It's akin to the case of "curiosity killed the cat."

The fact is, some risks promote very lopsided appraisals. Given high stakes, the cost of a false positive (playing it safe and looking a bit paranoid) can be much lower than the cost of a false negative (death because we ignored the threat). Sadly, System 1 is not very good at accurately judging the probability or severity of the risk, so false positives prevail and our body preps for a "fight or flight" response that doesn't differentiate between large or small risks. Evolution makes "tiger" the default setting on our threat-detection apparatus.[3] Playing it safe was quite adaptive when the cost of being wrong was a matter of life or death. But the stakes are rarely that high in the modern boardroom. Ironically, the costs of playing it safe are more likely to threaten our survival in the market or the firm.

We clearly need to retool our nervous system for the new world. Our environment has changed dramatically, even in the last 100 years, and the threats to our personal survival are not nearly so physical. But the evolution of our nervous system lags far behind, and physiologically, we are still at the stage of the "hunter-and-gatherer." We are still hard-wired to respond to uncertainty or newness by assuming the outcome will be dangerous or negative. We fear loss more than we appreciate gain, because our survival instinct kicks in any time we are confronted with uncertainty. As further proof that this tendency is instinctual, the same mechanisms have been observed in animals. Dogs, sheep, rats, starlings, and even honeybees have all been shown to have this same Cognitive Bias—perceiving uncertainty as threat. These studies also show that this tendency in animals to perceive novelty as negative increases when any amount of stress is added to the mix, just as it does in humans.

Since we cannot wait for evolution to "catch up" and modify the wiring of our brains, we need to take conscious control of the equipment we have inherited. While we cannot change the wiring (at least not much), we can modify the way the current flows through those archaic connections. This book is about taking control of what has become automatic and using it in a more adaptive and productive manner throughout the creative process of innovation.

In a time when social media prompts us to "Like" everything we see, why does negativity still persist in killing ideas? Because negativity sounds profound.[4] Important research from Teresa Amabile shows that book reviewers who tend to be more negative are perceived as more intelligent, competent, and expert than positive reviewers, even when the content of the positive review was independently judged as being of higher quality and greater forcefulness. According to this research, "a single instance of negative judgment might appear to result not from the narrow closed-mindedness of a limited intellect, but from the careful, incisive application of well-reasoned standards." Amabile states, "If the assessment is supported and elaborated at some length, the appearance of intelligence in a negative evaluator [will] be particularly strong." Now apply that to a room full of teams from disparate—sometimes even competing—factions of a company, and you may find that everyone is jockeying to be the smartest and most substantially negative person in the room. New ideas don't stand a chance.

So negative = smart. Yet since we have established that negativity is often the default, automatic mode, there is clearly a contradiction here. This isn't rational, but it's human.

Think back to a meeting you may have been in where someone was "naysaying" an idea. You may have noticed that the others in the room either joined in on the attack, or attacked the naysayer. In either case, "the nays have it." Negativity is contagious for evolutionary purposes. When one gazelle in the herd at the watering hole sees a lion, they *all* see the lion as the recognition spreads like a tidal wave. Those not paying attention get eaten.

In a group setting it can be difficult to singlehandedly shift the focus from "what you're against" to "what you wish for." In the high-stakes and potentially high-stress game of developing new products, processes, or business models, Negativity Bias is a significant factor that is almost certainly inhibiting your team's performance—and you're likely unaware of it.

Needless to say, what you say out loud matters. Especially when it comes to rejecting ideas. No one starts a project by saying, "I'm against new ideas." New ideas fuel discovery, change, and ultimately growth—but they also start with a whole lot of uncertainty. And it can be that uncertainty that subconsciously tanks a project from the get-go. One study titled "The Bias Against Creativity,"[5] looked at our deep-rooted negative perception of creativity and creative ideas, even when creative ideas were ostensibly sought. The research showed that people had a hard time understanding how novelty and practicality could go hand-in-hand. The more unique the idea, the more its usefulness was questioned—and ultimately, the perception of risk overcame the need for newness. Saying you want creativity yet inadvertently following your atavistic, albeit nonconscious instinct to reject the uncertainty of the new idea is dangerous in up-front innovation. According to this research, the bias against creativity is particularly problematic because people are not aware of what is driving their negative evaluations and therefore cannot correct for them.

We humans are incredibly skilled in finding the potential problems in any idea—whether it's at the front end of innovation or the back end—and everywhere in between along the innovation spectrum. So how does Negativity Bias rear its head in Opportunity ID, Ideation, and Concept Development? Into the breach!

NEGATIVITY BIAS ALSO EXPLAINS WHY WE TEND TO QUESTION our own ideas—and question others' ideas as well. It's essentially a two-gate system. New ideas either get one of the following:

- Discounted completely.
- Beaten into submission.

And then there's the case of "buyer's regret." You do all this research, and buy what you have always wanted, only to pick your choice to pieces, second-guessing every aspect of your decision under a wave of post-purchase negative appraisal.

The first way Negativity Bias affects new ideas is inside our own brain. It's like a monkey in our heads—leading us to overthink until it effectively cripples innovative thinking. When the task at hand is to generate new ideas during a brainstorming session, for example, Negativity Bias hampers progress in several ways.

- **Self-censorship**: Despite the innovation mantra of "fail often, fail fast, and fail cheap," few would say that failure is an integral element of their innovation strategy. People naturally like to succeed—and likewise are inclined to fear failure. So we censor our own ideas because of this unconscious fear of failure.

- **Self-doubt**, **also known as "I am not creative"**: This type of thinking holds people back. It kills the energy and participation and usually results in transforming creation into critique. It's actually avoiding work and passing the buck on a job everyone has a stake in, which is to *create* new ideas.

- **Insecurity or fear of looking stupid**: Here we see the perpetual Apologist where every idea is preceded with, "This isn't very good . . ." When someone is thinking this way, they will likely not participate in expansive thinking techniques or "wild" ideas, which will reduce both quantity and quality of ideas.

- **Perfectionism**: The perfectionists won't share until an idea is absolutely flawless. Meanwhile, they have a critical eye for imperfection and reject anything that's not up to their impossible standard. Needless to say, little gets generated.

The second way Negativity Bias works is in the way we react to the new ideas of other people. Since we are conditioned to perceive novelty as a threat, we tend to be suspicious of the new idea from the beginning. Then there's the self-serving appraisal of the amount of work involved and the probability of failure. And if those forces don't prompt us to preemptively kill the idea, we will certainly join in with any "nay-sayers" in the room. In such a risk-averse, negatively tuned environment, it's a wonder we can do any creative brainstorming at all that is outside the box of what is safe and conventional.

Again, many of these reactions arise from fear of failure and misunderstanding of what ideas are supposed to do for us early in the process. At this early phase, ideas should be golden nuggets that expand our thinking and promote discovery. When we err on the side of caution and believe that early-stage ideas need to be fully formed and complete, then we automatically lapse into judgment mode instead of discovery mode. To combat and preempt this natural tendency, each member of the group needs to make a point of proactively contributing half-baked, impractical, never-before-heard-of ideas—not because they are great ideas, but for the newness they'll create when engaged. You don't need to conduct an Ideation session to generate merely incremental, close-in ideas. Now is the time to push it, just to see where you can go.

Remember the metaphor from the Introduction—Negativity Bias is the pair of lead shoes we've all been walking around with. Slowing us down unnecessarily. Sucking too much energy out of us with little payoff. And yet we still get a lot of great things done! We've imagined ourselves as graceful, lithe dancers in this ballet and we've been Frankensteining it up rather comically—imagine the surplus of energy we'll have when we untie these shoes and take them off.

Negativity Bias in Opportunity ID

The smart, responsible-sounding quashing of Uniqueness starts here: "We know where we need to look . . . everyone in the industry knows what the opportunities are. We just need to execute on them better!"

Not so fast.

Your company and your brand mean something to your customers, whether you try to shape that meaning or not. Ultimately, despite all your marketing efforts, customers will position your company/brand in their mind in a way that makes sense to them. You need to understand what that distinct meaning space is for your product or idea and then follow it through either by building on it or by taking on the considerable effort to change it. If you're satisfied that your intent and your customer positioning match up, and that it is perspective that matters, you have a starting point for Innovation. You should consciously know what you're going to say "Yes!!!" to, what you're decidedly saying "No!" to, and what you're not going to pay attention to at all, or your nonconscious processes will prevail. When brand work is done right, your brand obviously carves out a space different from what anyone else in the category is standing for, because you understand the power of sacrifice in positioning and are "all in" on one big idea that's distinct from what your competitors have chosen.

Use that perspective to your advantage, and sharpen your pencil for some "Fill in the Blanks" work:

Because we're Brand _____ , we're going after big

opportunity areas that are more _____ , and less

_____ .

More _____ , less _____ .

More _____ , less _____ .

More _____ , less _____ .

We're going to over-deliver on _____ ,

while the rest of the category does it halfway.

We're not going to worry about _____ , because

the Brand _____ customer doesn't

really care about that.

Contrary to conventional industry wisdom, we choose to

_____ .

Even for category benefits such as _____ ,

our approach is _____—making it

more _____ , less _____ .

• • •

Differentiate, differentiate, differentiate! Even if certain category benefits are must-haves, find your POV on them. Flesh it out. Do the work.

For instance, we have heard for years that our clients' customers really want more convenience. Understood. Life's short. Let's get at it. But convenience, per se, is huuuuuuge! Break it down:

- A more _____ convenience
  (e.g., A more anticipatory convenience)
- Convenience that _____
  (e.g., Convenience that makes me confident)

Financial-services convenience isn't household cleaning convenience. And "Bank A" convenience should be noticeably different from "Bank B" convenience; otherwise, why bother marketing? Use this type of thinking to start driving new ways of approaching big opportunity areas. Avoid the "Yes, but . . . " reflex. As with all creative endeavors, come up with more opportunity areas than you can possibly cover, so you can converge on the best ones and start solving for Uniqueness (and the Relevance, right behind).

And remember, if where you start going sounds *realllly smart*, and yet it's bringing you back down to the category mean, you just might've fallen victim to Negativity Bias. In this specific application, smart can be stupid. Be truly smart by escaping the deadly clutches of Negativity Bias.

Negativity Bias in Ideation

While Negativity Bias can—and does—impact every stage of innovation, it is most prevalent and prominent in the idea generation phase. If you have ever participated in any type of idea generation, you have probably heard, or said, at least one or more of the following:

- It's too expensive.

- We've tried it before.

- That will take too long.

- "Helen" (or whoever is in the corner office) won't like it.

- We can't manufacture that product.

- Sales won't be able to sell that idea.

And the list could go on and on. In one twenty-minute training session with a client team, someone added to the above list, "We've never done it before." Between that novelty-killer, and "We've tried it before," we could just eliminate 100 percent of all new ideas and save ourselves a lot of work until we are completely unemployed.

We can think of a seemingly endless number of reasons why any idea might not work. Try it yourself. What's your initial gut reaction to each of these ideas?

- A refrigerator that actually grows the food inside.

- A car with triangle wheels.

- Condos that rotate like a Ferris wheel.

If you're like most people (and if you're being honest with yourself), you immediately thought each of these ideas was ridiculous. Your Negativity Bias (fueled by System 1 thinking) helped you to very quickly identify potential problems in each of these ideas and write them off as worthless. However, if you consciously suspend judgment for just a few seconds and begin to pick these ideas apart, there are some really interesting and potentially positive aspects within each of them.

- A refrigerator that grows the food inside might minimize wasted food. How could we create a refrigerator that minimizes the waste when food isn't eaten before it spoils?

- A car with triangle wheels would never roll down when parked on a hill. How might we use some feature of regular wheels to prevent inadvertent rolling downhill?

- Ferris wheel condos would allow each resident to feel like they have a penthouse suite, at least some of the time. In what ways could we build a penthouse-like feeling into all our condo units?

When we're educating client teams about Negativity Bias (and training them to avoid it), we frequently use an exercise that asks them to work in teams of two or three people and plan a party in three minutes—and we don't give them any guidelines. They can have any kind of a party they want: any theme, any music, any food or beverages, costumes or not. It's all open, with the exception of one rule: the only way anyone may respond to *any* idea or suggestion is to say, "Yes, and . . ." and then add to the idea. With only three minutes allowed for the exercise, most people assume there won't be enough time to plan anything—but the opposite is true. When the rule is that "there are no rules," people can come up with extremely interesting and fun ideas in an incredibly short amount of time. Most teams have a great party, with some very specific themes, beverages, music, and activities—fully formed and easily planned within the three minutes.

Then we repeat the exercise with the same group, but change the rule. They have to plan a different party, but this time, everyone must raise some potential objections by saying, "Yes, but . . . " followed by an objection or problem. We give them the same amount of time—just three minutes—then we have a discussion to compare and contrast the two processes and outcomes. Given the seemingly minor change of just one word—from "and" to "but"—the comments about the two processes are dramatically different.

When we ask people to share their observations about the "Yes, and . . . " process, nearly everything is positive. The observations people offered again and again include:

- It was fun!

- It was easy to come up with ideas.

- I was happy to participate.

- We built off each other's ideas.

- The party just kept getting better.

- It was incredibly productive (in the sense we got to a definitive plan very quickly).

- It felt like we were in "flow."

- It felt like real teamwork—everyone contributed and we worked well together.

- We came up with a great party that we'd all be excited to attend.

In fact, the experience is generally so positive for most people that we often have to overtly ask if there was anything bad about the "yes, and . . . " process before we hear anything negative. The primary negative we regularly hear is that the resulting party is out of reach in some way. Either it's too expensive, too difficult to implement, or just physically impossible, like the party on the moon planned by one client team. Because there were no limits, the ideas went over the top.

When we switch to discussing the "Yes, but . . . " experience, the energy is instantly sucked out of the room. We hear things like:

- We didn't get very far.

- I wanted to stop participating, or I *did* stop participating.

- It became argumentative.

- I felt like I had to defend every idea.

- Something that should have been fun felt like work.

- The "yes, but . . . " shut down every idea.

- Our party is boring and I wouldn't even go to it.

- We didn't even have a party, because we killed every idea.

The "yes, but . . . " experience is generally so negative for most people that we have to prompt them to consider whether anything about the process was positive. Some people say there was nothing positive about the experience. Others say the party they finally got to (if they got to one at all) was implementable, but boring.

So what's going on here? How can the substitution of one small word create such tremendously different scenarios? The answer is simply that in the "yes, and . . . " process, people were able to turn off their Negativity Bias, which resulted in more ideas, better ideas, and less judgment—which in turn leads to even more and better ideas. And, importantly, turning off the Negativity Bias creates an atmosphere that's more interesting, engaging, and fun, so people participate enthusiastically.

In the "yes, but . . . " process, we gave people permission to switch their Negativity Bias back on. Unfortunately, this is never hard for anyone to do. It is, after all, a very natural state for us, so we slip into it very easily. But, while it was great for the survival of our ancestors, it is a huge barrier for us today when we try to enact innovation and change. It stifles creativity, kills great ideas, and it creates such an unproductive, competitive, and somewhat hostile environment that people don't want to participate.

If Negativity Bias is so ingrained in us, why is it so easy for people to turn off their Negativity Bias in the "yes, and . . . " exercise?

There are a couple of reasons:

- They know it isn't real. They know they don't have to actually implement any of the ideas, so they don't have to worry about real world issues—like cost or feasibility.

- It reduces the risk and resulting stress that fuels the Negativity Bias. The greater the perceived risk and the higher the subjective stress, the more our Negativity Bias takes over to "keep us safe." So planning an imaginary party in a scenario where there's no risk makes it easier to let go of negativity. This wouldn't be the case if, for example, someone's job depended on the success of this party. If that were the case, it would have been much more difficult to let go of Negativity Bias.

So what's happening in our brain when we hear a new idea? We begin to break down that idea into parts so that we can assimilate it. We probably hear parts of the new idea that we like or that seem to make sense to us.

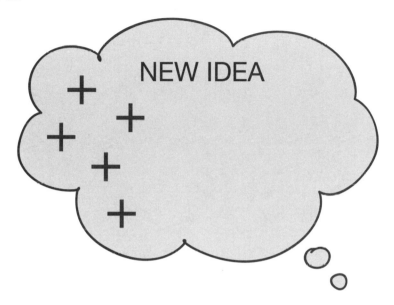

These are the parts we easily pick up on in the "yes, and . . . " scenario.

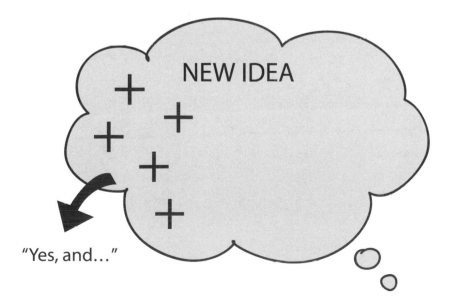

At the same time, however, we're also hearing parts we don't like, don't think will work, or don't completely understand.

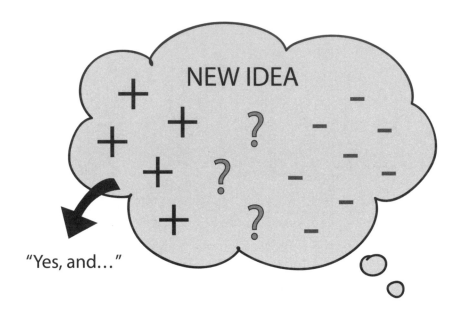

These are the parts we focus on in the "yes, but . . . " process—when our Negativity Bias kicks in. Research and our own experience have shown that groups are particularly effective at killing ideas using the "yes, but . . . " language.

So, when our goal is to create something new, it is imperative that we find a way to get past our individual and collective Negativity Bias. We need a process that gives us all the energy, flow, and willingness to participate that comes with the "yes, and . . . " process, but also allows us to acknowledge that every idea isn't perfect at first. We need to find another way of allowing critical thinking because "yes, but . . . " is not the way to do it. "Yes, but . . . " simply engages the Negativity Bias.

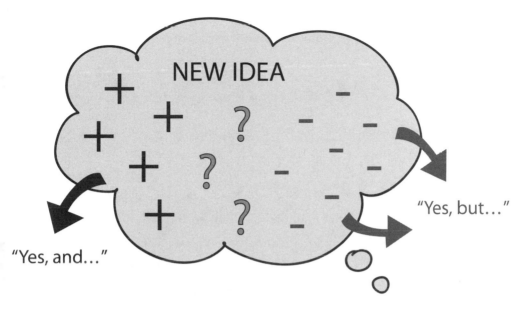

The most effective tool to get past Negativity Bias is the *Forness®* process, which emphasizes the skillful use of the word "*for.*" More than thirty-five years ago, Ideas To Go developed this thinking modality to combat Negativity Bias by emphasizing what people are in favor of, or "for," and what they "wish for." This became the novel quality of "for"ness. We teach this mental model to everyone who works with—and for—us to help them respond to new ideas in a way that illuminates the potential good in any idea, while acknowledging there are parts of the idea that still need work.

The *Forness* process is both an overt method to evaluate and optimize any individual idea and a simple way of thinking when new ideas are being generated or discussed. The process is actually quite simple and easy to learn, but yields a dramatically improved environment for innovation.

When you hear (or think of) a new idea, here is how to give it a *Forness* response:

1. Draw a large "T" grid on a piece of paper (see below).

2. In the upper left, write "FOR." In the upper right, write "WISH FOR ... "

3. In the left column, under "FOR," make a long list of many different aspects of what might be good, interesting, or valuable about this idea. It is important to make the list of "Fors" diverse, and have several items on the list. What you're trying to identify is the potential in the idea, knowing it's not yet finished. It still has some problems, which we will address in a moment. But assume, for now, that we can successfully address them, and focus on what is good about the idea. Don't stop after just one or two "Fors." The first ones tend to come easily and are obvious, so you need to keep pushing to get to the more provocative ones.

4. Now turn to the "WISH FOR" side of the sheet. This is not a list of "cons". While it does focus on the issues within the idea that may not be perfect, you need to use very specific problem-solving language to address them. Start every item on this list with either, "I wish ... " or "How to ... " or "How might we ... " or "In what ways might we ..."

Why is this language so important? It might seem like a very minor thing, but similar to the one-word difference between "Yes and ... " and "Yes, but ... ," this minor change in language has a dramatic effect on the process of innovation. The difference between "It costs too much" and "How might we reduce the cost?" makes all the difference. In the first instance, you're signaling your brain to throw that idea away because it's not workable. In the second mode of Ideation, you are signaling your brain to start problem solving. And the great news is that everyone who heard you say "How might we reduce the cost?" will also automatically start thinking of ways to join you in the problem-solving process. It's actually much easier than you might imagine to switch your brain from rejection mode to problem-solving mode. The Negativity Bias draws most of its power from its subconscious position. Once you get System 2 online, and train your brain to use techniques like the *Forness* process, you can direct the flow of creativity in new directions.

FORNESS RESPONSE

What you're for	What you wish for
THE WAY IT IS NOW	TO MAKE THE IDEA BETTER
• What's good	• I wish…
• What's useful?	• How to…?
• What's valuable?	• How might we…?
• What's the potential?	These words are critical.
•	STEP 1: Articulate the problem.
•	STEP 2: Generate solutions
•	STEP 3: Generate other ideas sparked by either side

The final step in the *Forness* process is to use the list of "WISH FORS" to generate potential solutions for the identified issues, or to generate new ideas that were sparked by the original idea, but don't have the same problems. We find that these solutions and new ideas may happen spontaneously and simultaneously while articulating the issues prompted by the problem-solving statements. Our experience is that people are generally pretty quick to start thinking of solutions and ideas as soon as they hear the problem-solving statement framed as "I wish . . . " or "How to . . . " Wishes can manifest as either productive restatements of the problem or as concrete solutions. This is more evidence that it is easier than you might think to redirect the workings of our mind once we consciously shift from the "automatic pilot" of System 1.

Now it's time for you to practice. At the top of the next page, you will find an idea that probably needs work. Using the T-grid on that page, do a *Forness* response to the idea. Remember that you always start with what you are "FOR," before you turn to what you "WISH FOR." So start by making a long list of aspects of that idea you could be "for." (And don't turn the page before you create your own.)

Once you've completed the left side with "FORS," use the right side of the page to identify the issues you see using the problem-solving stems "I wish . . . ," "How to . . . ," or "How might we . . . " (Tip: Saying "I wish this idea didn't suck" isn't what we're going for. We call that a "Yes, but . . . " in disguise.)

Now that you've framed what you believe to be the biggest issues with this idea, generate a few potential solutions, or other new ideas that occurred to you as you evaluated the original idea. You'll be surprised how easy it is to use these simple sentence stems to break through resistance and discover new possibilities. Keep in mind that you *are* allowed to change the original idea. In fact, you have to change it in order to optimize it. The point is to keep some of the interesting, unique, and valuable aspects that you noted on the "FOR" side, while modifying the idea to solve for the problems.

FORNESS Exercise

Here's the idea: a kitchen or bathroom sink made of fur (all credit to Steve Martin).

FORNESS RESPONSE

What you're for	What you wish for
THE WAY IT IS NOW	TO MAKE THE IDEA BETTER
•	•
•	•
•	•
•	•
•	•
•	•
•	•

How did you do? Did you identify some of the things we included on our list below? You probably even thought of things we didn't consider. That's why this process works well with a group—the collective power of the group to articulate what's good and to generate solutions for the issues is tremendous.

FORNESS RESPONSE

What you're for	What you wish for
THE WAY IT IS NOW	TO MAKE THE IDEA BETTER
• Soft for bathing baby or pet	• I wish it didn't smell like a wet dog
• Keeps the water hot longer	• How to clean it?
• Can use the fur as a scrubbing tool, like for under fingernails	• I wish it didn't hurt an animal to make it
• Can use the fur to dry my hands	• How to make it sanitary?
• Contacts won't slide down the drain	• How to get toothpaste out of it?
• Will hide beard shavings	
• Will hide dirt, so I have to clean less often	NEW IDEAS
• Dropped dishes or glasses won't break	• Faux fur sink
• Instantly updates my decor	• Sink made of glass, fur is under the glass
• It's trendy	• Special shampoo to easily clean the fur
	• Fur liner that is removable and washable
	• A new disposible liner each week, so I never have to clean my sink again!
	• A bathtub lined with a material that keeps the water hot longer

Humans have an almost unlimited capacity for solving problems. It's one of the things that make us human, once we make the shift from our more primitive and risk-averse System 1 thinking to our more thoughtful

System 2 mode of interacting with the world. Using the *Forness* process to flip the switch from the "Yes, but . . . " Negativity Bias to the "Yes, and . . . " problem-solving mode will often release a torrent of creative thinking that can be equally contagious in a group.

There are several benefits to the *Forness* process:

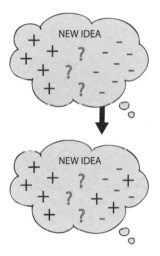

BENEFITS

1. Keeps the good alive

2. Pushes toward actionable solution

3. Creates a safe environment

4. Encourages teamwork and ownership

5. Saves time

- **It keeps the good alive**. Instead of instantly judging and throwing away an idea because it's not perfect, we consciously identify the good parts of an idea and maintain those parts in any modification or new idea that comes from it.

- **It drives toward practical solutions**. Many people have participated in brainstorming sessions where someone sets the ground rule: "Remember, every idea is a good idea!" Then there's usually a collective eye roll, because no one really believes that. The fact is, it's not actually true—and probably never will be. Not every idea is a good idea, and trying to force people to pretend differently isn't very realistic. You have to acknowledge the reality that not every idea is good, and even a good idea isn't perfect at the beginning. The *Forness* process works because it allows for the reality that most ideas need work before they become great ideas. This method helps optimize the initial ideas so they become great, because they're now both innovative *and* implementable.

- **It helps us feel safe** to share our ideas out loud in the group. As you recall from the prior discussion of the "Yes, but . . . " process when people plan a party, people often shut down when the environment allows for instant and open criticism of every idea. That's because no one wants to be "Yes, butted." It simply doesn't feel good. It's not fun, it's not productive, and it makes people feel like the rest of the group believes they are stupid. Even when you already know that your idea isn't perfect, having someone tell you that still isn't helpful. If you know that your colleagues will treat your idea in a *Forness* way by identifying the positive, and then help optimize your idea by articulating the problems in a more useful way, you're much more willing to share your ideas. When ideas are shared and the power of the group is harnessed to make them even better, amazing things will happen.

- **It builds a feeling of teamwork and increases commitment** to the ideas. If everyone feels like they contributed to an idea by identifying the issues and working together to optimize the idea, it has a much greater likelihood of survival, and the process is a more satisfying experience for everyone. This process will also help move the idea forward to success because everyone has some ownership and the idea has multiple champions.

- **It's incredibly efficient**. When less time is devoted to talking about why an idea won't work and more energy is devoted to identifying what's good, what needs to be solved for, and how to make the idea stronger by coming up with actual solutions, little time is wasted on unproductive rehashing of negativity. If it is ultimately determined that an idea can't become practical, it is easy to take the good aspects you've already identified and develop a different idea that will still have those good parts.

- **Bonus Point: It always—every time—results in sparking additional ideas**. So, even if the original idea is never going to work, it will likely have prompted two or three other ideas that just might be the solution you are looking for.

IMPROV RULES "YES, AND . . . "

"Yes, and . . . " is the cardinal rule of comic improvisation that leads to the wildly creative entertainment most people love. And not surprisingly, most of the rest of the rules of improv[6] are also applicable to innovation improvisation:

- Say Yes, and . . .
- After the "and" add new information
- Don't block
- Avoid questions
- Focus on the here and now
- Be specific—provide details
- Change, change, change
- Focus on characters and relationships
- Commit and take choices to the nth degree

One of the classic examples of "yes, and . . . " working well is in improvisational theater. "Improv" is a form of art that is creative, collaborative, instantaneous, and infectious (much like a well-run Ideation session). And while it looks like there are no rules onstage because of the unscripted nature of the performance, the improv structure would collapse if it weren't for a few key rules that keep the story going. The cardinal rule of improv is the use of "yes, and . . . ." By saying "yes, and . . . ," the story that the actors are building can move forward. By adding new information after the "and," the actors are free to explore a plot line all the way through. A scene is killed almost immediately when another actor fails to play by this rule— either denying the thread already woven onstage, or shutting down the story by asking questions or simply saying "no." For example:

"Do you see that bear over there?"

"No."

The end.

The story has nowhere to go once it's been shut down. Keeping the story alive in improv is like keeping the good alive in an idea. It may not start off as the best, most polished idea ever, but once you go in with a spirit of collaboration using the rules of improv, you end with improved ideas.

• • •

Remember that *Forness* thinking is not only a specific tool that you can apply to an individual idea, but perhaps more importantly, a mind-set that you need to adopt any time new ideas are being generated or discussed. Your default mode is the risk aversion of System 1. If you're in a brainstorming session, you don't need to write down a *Forness* response to every single idea that is generated. Instead, you simply need to keep the *Forness* mindset the whole time. Internalize it! If you hear an idea that just switched on your Negativity Bias and you can't get past it, write a *Forness* response to that particular idea. It might help you morph it into something that is still exciting, but now also workable. And even if the original idea can never be made practical, it will at least spark other interesting ideas to consider.

At Ideas To Go, we begin every idea-generation session by training the participants in *Forness* thinking. Even clients who've worked with us multiple times go through this process as a reminder/refresher because the Negativity Bias exists in all of us all the time, and it is a tenacious adversary. If we are not vigilant about consciously overcoming this fundamental bias, we will unwittingly fall back into safe mode. Despite many years of training others in this model, we are still prone to fall into the same trap. Hey, we're still human. Some of us have even taught the *Forness* mindset to our kids, only to be confronted by them when we "yes, but" them (seems unfair). So we constantly remind ourselves, our clients, and our employees about *Forness* thinking to keep switching off our own Negativity Biases.

We believe so strongly in the power of *Forness* thinking that we have created "No Yes, but . . . " stickers, buttons, and tattoos (temporary ones) as a visible reminder to use this mindset to keep our Negativity Bias at bay.

If you'd like some stickers for your team, you can get them at www.ideastogo.com. You'll also find a free downloadable *Forness* process worksheet you can use. We ask only that you maintain the Ideas To Go branding and copyright notice.

Negativity Bias in Concept Development

By this stage, you've come too far to let Negativity Bias back in. But it's tenacious and resourceful. During the Concept Development stage it tends to masquerade as "adult responsibility." The previous stages have more tolerance for ambiguity built in: *Ideation* is supposed to be all fun and whacky, and the *Opportunity ID* stuff is just so abstract, but *Concept Development* is where we are supposed to tighten things down and get real, right?

That sounds so reasonable. But it isn't.

Getting Real during Concept Development is about making smart choices for *learning purposes,* not for launch. It's so understandable that launch considerations come up prematurely—there's something really comforting about the concrete, and our business doesn't get paid for great learning, at least not directly. It's time for a little delayed gratification for the sake of a greater payout later.

Now is the time to lean in hard and get clarity on what you're really *for* out of all the possibilities generated during Ideation, and to work hard on what you *wish for* to pull it all together. Based on all the ideas you've generated, what would you like to learn via the concepts you're going to develop? Think of concepts you are about to develop at this stage as "individual learning vehicles" instead of launch candidates. They may very well make it to launch, but let's make that determination after maximizing the opportunities of each potential vehicle.

Another common case of Negativity Bias in Concept Development is the phenomenon of preemptively deciding for the customer: "Oh, they'll never go for that," or "I'm not sure our target is ready for that," etc., etc. There's a very easy way to rule out these concerns—test and find out. Perhaps the customer isn't ready for the full expression of Uniqueness in the idea as it stands at the moment; but what if going 60 percent toward it *does* hit the sweet spot of Uniqueness and Relevance for the customer? Maybe the idea at the moment is just too far ahead of the market, but a) you need some time to develop the product anyhow—the target is always moving, and b) you will never know if there is anything in this general direction that would be a potential "vein of ore" for you if you don't ask. Work on the idea in development to increase its potential, but let your customers tell you what else you need to learn about it. Cutting it off right now robs you of that. *Learning, not Launching!*

AN ARTICLE IN THE *MIT TECHNOLOGY REVIEW* RECOUNTS HOW the famous science fiction author Isaac Asimov was once invited to provide input to a US government project designed to elicit the most creative approaches possible for a ballistic missile defense system. He wrote an essay for the team outlining the critical elements needed in creative thinking. Way back in 1959, he identified both the Negativity Bias (using different words) and the need for an environment that fosters creativity, like the *Forness* response.

There must be ease, relaxation, and a general sense of permissiveness. The world in general disapproves of creativity, and to be creative in public is particularly bad. Even to speculate in public is rather worrisome. The individuals must, therefore, have the feeling that the others won't object.

For best purposes, there should be a feeling of informality. Joviality, the use of first names, joking, relaxed kidding are, I think, of the essence—not in themselves, but because they encourage a willingness to be involved in the folly of creativeness. For this purpose I think a meeting in someone's home or over a dinner table at some restaurant is perhaps more useful than one in a conference room.

We have found that creativity is more likely to bloom anywhere outside the conference room where you meet every day.

3

Availability Bias—What You See Is All There Is

AVAILABILITY BIAS IS A SHORTCUT OUR BRAIN TAKES TO HELP US make decisions more efficiently. Here's how Daniel Kahneman tees it up:

> We asked ourselves what people actually do when they wish to estimate the frequency of a category, such as "people who divorce after the age of 60" or "dangerous plants." The answer was straightforward: instances of the class will be retrieved from memory, and if retrieval is easy and fluent, the category will be judged to be large. We defined the availability heuristic as the process of judging frequency by "the ease with which instances come to mind."
>
> A question we considered early was how many instances must be retrieved to get an impression of the ease with which they come to mind. We now know the answer: none. For an example, think of the number of words that can be constructed from the two sets of letters that follow.

XUZONLCJM

TAPCERHOB

You knew almost immediately, without generating any instances, that one set offers far more possibilities than the other, probably by a factor of 10 or more. Similarly, you do not need to retrieve specific news stories to have a good idea of the relative frequency with which different countries have appeared in the news during the past year (Belgium, China, France, Congo, Nicaragua, Romania . . .). The availability heuristic, like other heuristics of judgment, substitutes one question for another: you wish to estimate the size of a category or the frequency of an event, but you report an impression of the ease with which instances come to mind.[1]

What immediately comes to mind provides the criteria for our decision making in most situations. And what easily comes to mind tends to be our most recent or emotionally charged memories, often at the expense of a more balanced or representative sample of the considerations we would select if we had the time. Many of the tasks of daily living simply don't require any extra level of analysis—automatic pilot works just fine. It's so easy, and yes, smart, to stick with the tried-and-true for most minor decisions—and it works perfectly well, as long as your world doesn't change and the stakes aren't very high.

As Phil McKinney says:

The problem that many business people, entrepreneurs, and would-be innovators suffer from is our inability to escape from our past. Simply put, we are all shaped by our past experiences, whether good or bad. We look at the end results of these experiences—"this idea worked"; "this idea failed"—and consciously or unconsciously turn these results into the rules by which we operate in the present. Sometimes these rules, or assumptions, are smart and valuable. However, the problems begin when we forget that these rules are a snapshot of an old paradigm or set of circumstances. In many cases, the world has moved on, but we are still clinging to the "obvious" ideas that were once true in the rapidly receding past. In order to progress, we need to learn to identify and ignore these "obvious" rules, ideas, or beliefs, and make room for a future where the rules are constantly being rewritten.[2]

When it comes to sorting through the considerations for most of our routine decisions, the loosely assembled "junk drawer" of availability in our head may be more than enough to draw upon. It's amazing what you can do with a little mental "duct tape" when you are too rushed or too lazy to look for a more sophisticated tool. But the Availability Bias is more pernicious than improvising with what is available. It also shapes our definition of the world and dramatically limits what we believe is possible within it. As Kahneman explains, we usually operate as if "What you see is all there is."[3] Our unique capacity for problem solving works against us when we assume that any problem can be solved by using what we have on hand. As the old adage goes, "When all you have is a hammer, everything is treated like a nail." And in many cases, a hammer will do just fine.

But the most easily retrievable inputs and memories aren't always the most reliable or representative. Since emotionally charged memories are more vivid, and vivid memories are more easily retrieved, emotion trumps reason when the Availability Bias is in play. For example, brides often buy the first wedding dress they try on because it's the first time they visualize themselves as a bride. That first experience in a wedding dress brings out so many strong emotions that they tend to return to that dress even after trying on other dresses that might have been preferred if the emotion-laden Availability Bias hadn't short-circuited their decision making.

And from what we know about Negativity Bias, the power of a few bad memories will outweigh more numerous good ones. They are also more easily retrieved.

The metaphor for Availability Bias in the Introduction was blinders, such as on a horse. We've been the dedicated beasts of burden in high-traffic areas with blinders on to keep us trotting forward. Taking a moment to consider a little more won't steer us into the ditch. Taking a little more time up front to look at more, selected in a smart, strategic way, will actually speed up time to market acceptance.

Like the Negativity Bias, Availability Bias appears in many phases of the innovation process.

Availability Bias in Opportunity ID

The task of Opportunity Identification in the innovation process is to define a territory where your brand/product has the potential to meet your customers' needs in a way that over delivers benefit to them and maximizes profit to you. We're hunting for the intersection of (1) something that's clearly important to the customers and (2) for your offering to deliver benefit in a way that makes a remarkable—or even indispensable—difference to those customers. When that's something that's obvious *only* in hindsight, you have hit pay dirt, and have set up a powerful platform to get the "separate yourself from the pack" power of Uniqueness coupled with "really fits in my life" Relevance.

That's why the Availability Bias in Opportunity Identification is both understandable and vexing. You're already behind on the next big idea, and now you have to spend time trying to figure out where to go next. The sales people have already told you what your customers are screaming for—so get going! Industry events announce months in advance what the hot areas are. Big macro-trends across categories are in your face daily. There's no shortage of people who believe they know precisely where you need to go next.

How should you be thinking about Opportunity ID? When everyone else is zigging, maybe it's time to zag. What different questions should you be asking at this stage that you wouldn't ask downstream? You begin to overcome the inertia of Availability Bias when you ask different questions. As innovation author Stephen Shapiro says, "Don't think outside the box; get a better box!"[4]

One way to get a "better box" is to set up a very different contextual experience to stimulate very different thinking. We were fortunate to work with a major consumer-products company that wanted to understand a big new opportunity area in a fresh, non-obvious way. Managers from three of their huge consumer brands wanted to make sure they were really diving deeply and thinking differently from anyone else in the category before each brand went off to do innovation work.

We took up the challenge to stretch their thinking, and developed a rich, experiential round-robin panel of experts who could provide them with a compelling experience and comment on their new opportunity area in individual ways. The approach is "Diverse by Design," where we consciously choose perspectives to cover more of the opportunity landscape, rather than just throwing eclectic perspectives in the mix for the sake of being eclectic. We set up the "stations" with each of the following experts who would help our clients consider their new opportunity from each of these deliberately distinct perspectives:

- A Zen priest
- A music therapist
- A massage therapist
- A food scientist (note: it wasn't a food project!)

Each "turn" began with twenty minutes of experiential stretching, followed by a moderated dialogue about the experience for another twenty-five minutes to capture impressions, quarter-baked suppositions, thoughts that had just never occurred to them before, etc. We were careful to preempt any premature momentum into product or communication possibilities—this was about fertilizing and tilling the soil, perhaps planting some seeds, but creating the best mental and experiential conditions for these managers to escape the pull of the obvious as they later went forward to innovate. And it was more fun than geeky innovationistas should ever be allowed to have.

Day Two was all about processing these experiences and finding big, broad themes, "aha moments," insights, and smaller opportunity spaces within the broader opportunity umbrella—all still operating at the fresh conceptual level, with no pressure to move into product or communication possibilities quite yet.

Nothing here "cured" the managers of any future Availability Bias—the experience merely gave them some great new, easily summoned (read: "Available") memories that will be more provocative and helpful during their innovation.

REMEMBER THAT THE BIASES WE'RE DISCUSSING ARE DEEP, millennia-old features of human cognition—not easily "cured," but we can use the predictability of their very nature to lessen their negative impact. Arm yourself for Availability Bias coming up later by having more vivid "stretch experiences" that will, by their exciting nature, be more memorable and therefore accessible. For Availability Bias, it's about creating better, more conscious, shorter cycles of input and recall. Recall of better stimuli and the associations that always come with them will help move you forward.

You start innovation off right in Opportunity ID when you deliberately set up different thinking and doing for the various mental, experiential needs of this stage of development. This should vary even from your best thinking and behavior in Ideation and Concept Development, and differ from the way you think during full-on solution mode while in Product Development.

If the knowledge needs are different during the stages of innovation, one helpful approach to understanding the unique knowledge needs is provided by borrowing the Johari Window construct from psychology.

The Johari Window is a tool that helps people better understand their relationship with themselves and others by using a four-quadrant "window." The original focus was on two axes—What I Know About Myself (or not), and What Others Know About Me (or not). We tweak it for our purposes here to map out the Knowledge Journey, with additional axes labeled What We Know (or don't), and What We're Aware Of (or not). Innovation can be thought of as this Knowledge Journey, going from the Unknown to the Known.

In Opportunity ID, we start the journey from a place we commonly see in client companies, the Unknown Knowns—meaning we don't know collectively what we know individually. Opportunity ID focuses on the first two quadrants: (1) We Don't Know (collectively) What We Know (individually) and (2) We Don't Know What We Don't Know.

1. *We Don't Know (Collectively) What We Know (Individually).* Often, obscured pockets of knowledge exist within the organization that could be helpful right up front: "Someone did work on this three years ago . . . didn't I hear that?" "Hey, Janice has that report from last year that overlaps with what we need here, right?" *Expose* this knowledge to those who will be working on a particular effort. Active Knowledge Transfer among team members will move you forward. The key is *Active* Knowledge Transfer. Many knowledge transfer processes simply attempt to convey facts. Active Knowledge Transfer will help you move beyond "Oh, that's good to know," to "Hey, maybe we can use this information in this particular way."

By sharing knowledge across structural and inadvertent boundaries within a group or organization, this synthesizing of potential aha moments, implications, and illustrative possibilities will move the innovation process forward more dramatically than simply sharing facts. After this, you'll have a better sense of what you need to accomplish next.

1. *We Don't Know What We Don't Know.* This is the time to *experiment* with various approaches to see what emerges in context. We're looking for those things that you couldn't have thought of until you're in the moment of truth. This is the realm of emergence that is facilitated by various methodologies, including Ideas To Go's *Creative Ethnography* service and other approaches that will help you form better questions and differentiate areas to explore.

By working through these two quadrants in this way, you will be in a much better position to avoid the pitfalls of the Availability Bias in the Opportunity Identification stage.

The stages of Ideation and Concept Development can make effective use of the last two quadrants of the Johari window.

2. *We Know What We Don't Know.* During the Ideation stage, it's time to *explore* specific, broad opportunity areas to see what specific, illustrative possibilities might look like within each. You'll get the Unique, Relevant building blocks you need for the next step of concept development and testing.

3. *We Know What We Know.* In this quadrant we can start to *exploit* specific opportunities, getting into product development and building the profit plan.

More on these last two later in this chapter.

By working through the Johari Window during Opportunity Identification, you can help overcome Availability Bias by uncovering hidden opportunities in a short amount of time.

THE JOHARI WINDOW

A model to identify knowledge buckets and gaps. Each quadrant has a different need, and therefore a different activity to address it.

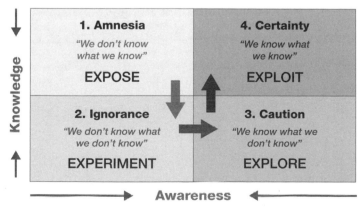

Using stimuli—like the kind generated through the Johari Window—throughout Opportunity ID helps you escape the limitations of Availability Bias. Specific ID/discovery exercises help, and here are four of the most important:

- **Insight Mining**—Including consumer insights research, digital digs, and Forness–style "wishing."

- **Category Crashing**—Surveying what's already in the target market, adjacent markets, and even completely different markets.

- **Trend Hunting**—Including examining mega-shifts and trends.

- **Tech Search**—Reviewing technology of supplier partners, existing inventions, academic articles/authors, patent searches, etc.

Caveat: These don't give you the answer! Done well, they create the necessary preconditions where more promising and differentiating opportunities can come out.

In our experience, using lots of stimuli dramatically increases a team's effectiveness early in the innovation process. You have more pathways to explore, more opportunities to exploit, and more ways to make your brand/product matter more.

It is equally important to use a system of stimulus mining that is quick and easy. Otherwise, you are unlikely to find the time to devote to this very important phase of the innovation process. It has to be fast and easy, or our best intentions don't quite get us there. We won't do it if it's arduous.

Here's why you need to take the time to fight Availability Bias in Opportunity ID. Think for a moment what "bet" you're making if you simply go with the flow. You're trusting current customers with current needs to determine your future. They're selfish (as they should be) and focused on immediate gratification. It's not their job to forecast what they'll want in the future. Most of them don't know how their needs are evolving. They're busy and preoccupied. They want you to stay right where you are, to be a good, consistent commodity that solves their problems as they exist now. Their current needs are important now, and you're smart to address them now, but you can't stop there, or you'll be left behind as the market evolves without you. Regular "Voice of the Customer" work brings you current Relevance, but not much Uniqueness, nor what will emerge as Relevant later. Now is the time to think about gaining the competitive advantage.

Someone in your market is going to be the first to address emerging needs. That's where the profit is. One study shows that a comprehensive corporate strategy of Innovation (vs. the alternative strategies of low cost, quick delivery, voice of the customer, and high quality) resulted in the highest profit margin, doubling the return from low cost and improving upon the others by 40 to 50 percent.[5] Is there a particular reason it shouldn't be you who takes the Innovation lead in your category?

Your company and your brand should be making bets on the future different from those made by the competition. Ideally, you have positioned your offering sharply, sacrificing *everything* you could say about it in order to reap the benefits of specific focus and the claims you can make within that focus. You're actively creating your choice of a future that differs from that of your competition if you've effectively connected your positioning to strategy and execution. Category table stakes or cost-of-entry features matter, but they're not all that matters, and they will quit being table stakes at some point. Today's delighters become the next round's table stakes, and as an innovation practitioner, you're in the business of creating delighters or future table stakes. As former Apple Fellow Alan Kay said, "The best way to predict the future is to invent it."

You take the first step toward Uniqueness and Relevance when you make sure that you're playing in an arena where your Uniqueness and distinct perspective on Relevance have more room to breathe.[6] Go where you increase the likelihood of being truly remarkable—or even better, indispensable. Stack the deck in your favor. Opportunity ID is the first opportunity you have to write different rules of competition. Lapse into default category expectations here and you've already given up too much ground to the competition. Now is the time to make it as difficult as possible for your competitors to gain any ground on valuable customer-need space.

It helps if you're the first to discover and define some new need space.

Of course, marketers know they have to be different. The fact is, so does everyone else. Being different is just not enough anymore. It is an incredibly complex marketplace. In any one grocery store, there are approximately 38,000 SKUs—more than double the number of just a few years ago. As product and service developers, we are prolific. But propagation does not ensure survival. Being merely different means your product may just outlast its shelf mates, and that's it. Stretching beyond differentiation to being remarkable is better. At least being remarkable puts you in a smaller subset of standouts. It's when you push so far out that you become indispensable—that's when you hit the mark. You are the start of a new list, a new category, a new star creating a new solar system around it.

Think that's too over-the-top? Think about how the Digital Video Recorder (DVR) changed how an entire generation understands and consumes content (and then consider the fate of the previous innovators who rested on their laurels). The notion that an entire population would sit down and watch the same thing on television at the same time is unheard of these days. By reimagining how people can watch what they want, when they want, it also launched complementary and adjacent products and services to be consumed with the new technology.

This is not to say that the DVR created the mobile device; but it opened up an entire new realm of possibilities by supposing people did not have to be tied to their TVs at a particular time. It also forced many industries such as consumer packaged goods, insurance, and financial services to rethink how they put their products and services in front of consumers who no longer sit through commercials.

The task is to capture all the apparent Relevance in a way that isn't trite. What if our starting points, the insights that set the stage for our innovation to matter, were obvious in a nonobvious way? As we stated at the beginning of the chapter: What if they were *obvious only in hindsight?*

Insights that are obvious only in hindsight, and that set the stage for your offering to matter more, are where we want to explore; and that takes focus. It's not entirely like threading a needle while riding on the back of a Harley during a hurricane, but it does require a lot of awareness. The deck may be stacked against us, but if the game were too easy, it would be boring.

> **WEBSTER DEFINES AN INSIGHT AS "THE ABILITY TO PERCEIVE** the true or hidden nature of things." For our work in innovation, Ideas To Go defines insight as "The ability to perceive the true or hidden nature of things *in a way that drives to an opportunity to separate your product/brand from competitive pressures."*

You will not get there if you're considering only those things that everyone else in the category is considering. Somewhere between entrenched category assumptions and a net that's cast so wide that no one can manage the catch is some very promising territory to play with. And it doesn't have to be as difficult or time-consuming as you might think.

A good way to break away from the Availability Bias in Opportunity ID is to design the right mix of related and unrelated stimuli. By "design," we don't mean to make this sound hard, but to make it clear that some thoughtfulness in the prep of stimuli pays dividends. The stimuli you'll find helpful in Opportunity Identification should be different from those you pull together for Ideation; it's going after bigger game. But it's still helpful to make sure you're getting both related stimuli and unrelated stimuli, so you prime your brain for both Relevance and Uniqueness.

We define *related stimuli* as information directly relevant to your topic or challenge in some way. *Unrelated stimuli* are simply new and different fodder—purposely *not* related to your topic—that will stimulate new thinking. For example, we partnered with a skin care company that was working on redefining the initial customer experience with its brand. We invited a panel of experts to share some knowledge in their own areas of expertise, to help expand the client team's thinking. We heard from a fashion designer, a plant historian, and a doctor who specializes in anti-aging (to speak on topics unrelated to anti-aging skin care). The contributions of these experts served to prompt our clients to begin to view their opportunities in new ways, which they readily acknowledged wouldn't have been possible without this unrelated stimulus. The use of stimuli like this in Opportunity ID can push your thinking about your challenge in bigger, broader ways.

Availability Bias in Ideation

In Ideation, we employ Excursion Theory to address the Availability Bias. Without some sort of "mental excursion," you are prone to go with the first thing that comes to mind. Excursions are consciously off-topic, guided exercises that force your mind to diverge from the beaten track. This detoured thinking allows you to come up with new areas of opportunity that might never have seen the light of day if you relied solely on what was immediately available to your brain. Once you push beyond familiar ways of thinking, you get to ideas that are original and imaginative. You can then apply Forness thinking to make them usable and practical. In Excursion Theory, there really is no such thing as stretching too far—it's always easier to make a wild idea possible than to make an old or boring idea exciting. It's a good rule of thumb to "Solve for Uniqueness" first, then bring in additional Relevance as needed.

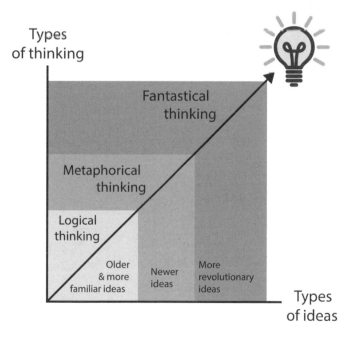

Here's how it works:

- We are trained to think logistically and analytically, but that will take you only so far in the world of innovation.

- Metaphorical thinking takes you to the next level. It gets you to communicate a new idea by borrowing from a familiar category—helping you see beyond what something is, to what it's like, and could be like.

- Eventually, you push further out to even wilder ideas.

- The final step is to bring the idea back into the realm of possibility (through Forness thinking, from Chapter 2) and to see the idea more clearly—how it fits your objectives and the realities of the world.

Recall from above the discussion about using both Related and Unrelated stimuli. You need both to get Uniqueness and Relevance. In Ideation, it is important to make more stuff (a technical term) available for your mind to play with. Fresh stimuli will summon different memories and associations. Use cycles of stimulus and recall to help you and to make richer ideas available to you.

Here's a great excursion to blast through Availability Bias by using the power of complete randomness:

Chain of Associations

1. Get all the Ideators together in a line, facing the Facilitator.

2. Have the Facilitator give an entirely random word to the first person in the line, such as "chicken" (assuming here we're not working on an exciting new chicken offering).

3. Give the first person no more than two seconds to shout out anything that comes to mind. Don't overthink it. It's actually better if it's not too linear. The first person's gut reaction to "chicken" could be "colonel," "car contest," "noodle," "lickin'," or "Tadzhikistan"

(that's a specific recipe for chicken . . . right? It came up in my mind for some odd reason!),

4. Have the next person associate to the last word heard. Think quickly! The response to "Tadzhikistan" could be "adventure travel," "tahini" (c'mon, it kinda sounds like the prompt!), "history," "stannous fluoride," . . . whatever. No need to defend the response. Random is good. Have some fun—there should be some laughs throughout.

5. Have the Facilitator or someone else write down each response in large letters on a flip chart. (Pro tip: alternate marker color on each response to increase legibility and make it colorful)

6. Do a couple of rounds—get at least twenty free associations up on the chart.

7. Break into pairs or trios and randomly pick one of the responses on the chart, force-associate it to the topic or Target Area you're working on at the moment, and see where it goes. For example, if we were working on "New Eating Occasions for Gelatin" and if I picked "noodle" from the list, I'd start playing with interesting new forms and viscosities of the gelatin that would still give me great, refreshing gelatin flavors but maybe with slightly different textures. A pack of gelatin worms in four different flavors for a fun afternoon protein snack? Hey . . . I know some kids of all ages who would give that a try.

Use the very first ideas that come up more for their provocative value rather than their immediate launch-worthy merits. These early ideas are certainly not end destinations in themselves, but vehicles to take you to promising new territory you never thought of before. Keep pushing further and avoid rushing to solutions. Go one, two, even three levels out from the first idea and create a healthy multiple of it—see how quickly a great "stretch idea" turns into a dozen solid ideas.

Here's a metaphor for you. All manufacturers use raw materials in the production of their final products. We don't judge the raw materials by the standards that we would for final consumption or use. I don't expect cacao nibs to be as delectable as the final dark chocolate bar I'm going to enjoy. But I don't get to the delectation without the admittedly funky-tasting (note: and funky-smelling) nibs early on. There's little in the great final product that is predictable from the weird, yeasty, pungent olfactory blast that one gets wafting off the woven-cane mats where the cacao beans dry.

Same thing with the best ideas. If you're asking the earliest ideas to hop over the hurdles for the final product, you're going to miss out on the richest potential. Appreciate ideas early on for their provocative value rather than for their immediate merits.

Pro tip: Between voting on your plethora of ideas and championing the best ones to set up Concept Development, take a moment to regroup and talk about Key Takeaways from Ideation. This facilitated discussion helps the group focus on more than just the last thing they read or heard. Instead, the discussion warms up System 2 thinking to come back on line.

Availability Bias in Concept Testing

Now that you've found the right mix of concepts worth developing, the next Availability Bias "watch out" is during Concept Testing.

We know there are lots of ways to test concepts. The one we're going to focus on here is one of the most useful methods when it is done right:

focus groups. The typical focus group process has a moderator in a room with your target customers talking about each concept one at a time, while you—the brand and market research team—watch from a back room. If it's like most moderated focus groups, they are run in a series so you can get the most customer feedback in the shortest amount of time. That's a lot of data to remember and process—especially when the analysis of all that output directly affects where you put your company's time, money, and resources. If you wait until later to recall what was said, the Availability Bias may kick in, and you may miss key learning and insights that your brain didn't file as Most Memorable.

Instead of waiting to talk about what you heard during focus groups, try a more active process. We developed *Live Takeout*™ as a process to prompt more effective and efficient discussions of customer feedback. During focus groups, we lead work teams in a discussion about insights and implications immediately after each idea is discussed—while everything is fresh in your mind. The document created from this serves as the foundation for a Final Learning and Takeout Discussion.

Availability Bias in the Development Phase

The threat of Availability Bias extends into the Development phase when we are thinking through potential solutions and often miss information or ideas that might help make better decisions. As we encounter challenges throughout the development process, we rely on our past experience and knowledge to solve new problems. We tend to solve each new problem in the same ways that have worked with similar issues in the past. This approach may be practical, but it is hardly innovative, and it clearly limits the likelihood of coming up with better solutions. It's hard for us to even realize that a new solution is needed or possible when the old solution is so readily available and compelling. It takes discipline to keep the creative juices flowing.

Using deliberate creativity techniques will help you come up with new ideas. Things like: getting outside your own conference room, debriefing the latest research in an art museum, or sending your team to the zoo with the objective of coming back with new ideas for the challenges you face. We frequently send client teams to the Mall of America, Walt Disney World, or a trendy area of Manhattan to look for inspiration and new ideas. If you can't physically get out of the building, then find a way to get out metaphorically. Ask people to imagine how they would solve the problem at hand if they lived in Antarctica, or if viewed from the perspective of a submarine captain, or if they were blind. This type of role-play is another example of Excursion Theory. And there's plenty of research that explains why it works so well.

Dr. Stephanie Carlson, an expert on brain development at the University of Minnesota, has demonstrated that imaginative role-playing boosts creative problem solving, even in unrelated areas. In her study, kids were randomly assigned to one of two conditions: (1) Pretend you're someone else (like Batman or Rapunzel) including wearing costume or using a prop or (2) Think really hard about your own thoughts and feelings. Then, the all the kids were asked to do the same problem-solving task. The kids who'd been instructed to pretend they were someone else performed significantly better in the creative problem-solving task, even when they were "out of character."

Dr. Carlson concluded that practice in pretending helps one come up with alternative ways of seeing an issue and results in more creativity and better problem solving.

We're not suggesting that creative problem solving is about ignoring facts; fact-finding and research are critical elements in the creative process at every phase. But so is imagination. To get to innovative ideas and solutions, we have to repeatedly toggle between analysis and synthesis, or between reality and possibility. The following excerpt from a *Newsweek* article entitled "The Creativity Crisis" describes what's happening in the brain during creative thinking:

> To understand . . . requires first understanding the new story emerging from neuroscience. The lore of pop psychology is that creativity occurs on the right side of the brain. But we now know that if you tried to be creative using only the right side of your brain, it'd be like living with ideas perpetually at the tip of your tongue, just beyond reach.
>
> When you try to solve a problem, you begin by concentrating on obvious facts and familiar solutions, to see if the answer lies there. This is a mostly left-brain stage of attack. If the answer doesn't come, the right and left hemispheres of the brain activate together. Neural networks on the right side scan remote memories that could be vaguely relevant. A wide range of distant information that is normally tuned out becomes available to the left hemisphere, which searches for unseen patterns, alternative meanings, and high-level abstractions.
>
> Having glimpsed such a connection, the left brain must quickly lock in on it before it escapes. The attention system must radically reverse gears, going from defocused attention to extremely focused attention. In a flash, the brain pulls together these disparate shreds of thought and binds them into a new single idea that enters consciousness. This is the 'aha!' moment of insight, often followed by a spark of pleasure as the brain recognizes the novelty of what it's come up with.

Now the brain must evaluate the idea it just generated. Is it worth pursuing? Creativity requires constant shifting, blender pulses of both divergent thinking and convergent thinking, to combine new information with old and forgotten ideas. Highly creative people are very good at marshaling their brains into bilateral mode, and the more creative they are, the more they dual-activate."[7]

There are lots and lots of tools and techniques that innovation consultants and creativity experts use to help people think differently and problem solve more creatively. But the easiest technique that anyone can employ at any time is simply to pretend. And another study has shown that it can work as well with adults. Darya Zabelina and Michael Robinson of North Dakota State University gave two groups of adult graduate students the same instruction. Both groups were told:

"School is canceled, and you have the entire day to yourself. What would you do? Where would you go? Who would you see?"

However, the instruction to one group began with the statement, "You are seven years old." Both groups had ten minutes to write down their answers, followed by several tests of creativity. The people who were "primed" to pretend they were seven-year-olds showed significantly higher levels of creative originality.

Availability Bias is all about selective recollection and the use of any data that is easiest to recall, including experiences, information, and memories. Role-playing (pretending) helps you get out of your own head and your own selective recollection, and lets you to recall or create other input that you can now bring to bear on a novel challenge.

The Scary Side Effects of Availability Bias

A marketing person from a food and beverage company shared samples from his development trial with his next-door neighbor, and the neighbor didn't like the flavor. He took this most alarming feedback back to his team and told them to "fix" it. This one person's casual feedback put the entire product launch in jeopardy, even though she was not considered the target audience.

It seems illogical that one person with no role in the decision process would have the deciding vote, but this happens more frequently than anyone wants to admit. The feedback was negative and it was emotionally laden, since it was provided by a personal friend; so it inadvertently became the most "available" input and primary decision-criteria for this marketing person.

4

The Curse of Knowledge—Well, It's Just Obvious that . . .

"Explain it to me like I'm a six-year-old."
—The character Joe Miller in *Philadelphia*,
portrayed by Denzel Washington

IN ADDITION TO SOME ENGAGING SELF-DEPRECATION, THIS LINE HELPS this character blast through layers of assumption and get to something that makes sense in a given situation.

There's something to be said for this approach in innovation.

As Mark Twain said, "It ain't what you don't know that gets you into trouble. It's what you know for sure that just ain't so." Elaborating on Twain may spoil his pithy prose, but let's go for it in the service of exploring the Curse of Knowledge—"It's what you know *but have no reasonable expectation that your customer would or should know* that gets you in trouble." It's not the customer's job to know the category as deeply as you do. *They* don't work for you. Sadly, they *don't* eat, breathe, and sleep your product or category. It might be very important to them, but you think about it more than your most rabid consumers.

The Curse of Knowledge makes it extremely difficult for someone with topic expertise to think about that topic from the perspective of someone with less knowledge. We all suffer from the Curse of Knowledge whenever we have any sort of experience within a subject, and even more so when we have any level of expertise. No matter how hard we try, or how much we believe we can mentally put ourselves in the place of "not knowing," we simply cannot do it.

When we were discussing how best to illustrate this phenomenon, one of our colleagues told us the following anecdote.

My grandmother was an expert bridge player. She was acknowledged by everyone who knew her to be, without a doubt, the best bridge player in their acquaintance. So, one evening after a family dinner, my brother, sister-in-law, and I asked her to teach us how to play bridge. We assumed this would be a wonderful experience—to learn from a master.

Unfortunately, the opposite turned out to be true. The entire experience was a debacle. My grandmother may have been an excellent bridge player, but she was a horrendous bridge teacher. It was an exercise in frustration for all of us. I didn't know why at the time, but now I understand that she was suffering from the Curse of Knowledge. Some things that would have been helpful for us to know were so second nature to her that it didn't occur to her that they even needed to be mentioned. And when we would ask questions, she would give explanations that made sense to her (with her knowledge), but made absolutely no sense to us.

I remember a specific example that got so ridiculous it became almost surreal. She was telling us that it was good to have only one card in a given suit. When we asked why, she answered, "Because it's a singleton." We said, "What's a singleton?" She said. "It's when you only have one card in a suit." When we asked why that's good—to have only one card in a suit—she replied that "It's because it's a singleton." This circular conversation got repeated a few times, much to the frustration of all of us. Finally, another relative who had been overhearing the conversation came to our aid and explained in terms we could understand why a singleton was good. After the explanation, my grandmother, who was in a bit of a huff by this time, exclaimed, "Well, of course that's why! Everyone knows that!"

This is the perfect example of the Curse of Knowledge; when you are expert in something, you are simply not consciously aware of all the things you know that other people don't know. It just doesn't occur to you that other people might not know these things, because they are so basic to you. And you don't recognize it. It simply isn't in your awareness. You can never unknow what you know and truly put yourself back in the position of being naive.

To experience this yourself, try this exercise developed by Elizabeth Newton, a grad student at Stanford, in 1990:

Think of a simple song that everyone knows, like "Mary Had a Little Lamb" or "Twinkle, Twinkle, Little Star." Now, find another person, and use a pen or pencil to tap out the rhythm of the song for the other person. Ask that person to guess the song by listening only to the tapping—no humming, singing, or lip-synching the words. *But first*—before you start, make a prediction about how likely you think the person is to guess correctly. It's a simple song, right? Everyone knows it, right? If you're like most people, you'll probably predict a fairly high likelihood that your listener will guess correctly. Now, go tap and have them guess.

How did they do? They guessed wrong, right? How do we know they guessed wrong? Elizabeth Newton proved that most people will not guess correctly. In the original experiment, 120 songs were tapped and only 3 listeners correctly identified the song being tapped. That's a 2.5 percent success rate.

However, the tappers had predicted, on average, a 50 percent chance the listener would guess correctly. So they dramatically overestimated the success rate. Why? Because of the Curse of Knowledge. For the tappers, it was impossible for them to unknow the melody and the words to the song. They couldn't unlink that knowledge in their heads to realize that the listeners would be hearing only a series of monotone sounds. Without the context of the melody and the words for the listeners, it's a bit like having just a few unconnected pieces of a jigsaw puzzle with no idea what the picture is supposed to be. But the tappers had all the pieces of the puzzle in their mental warehouse, so it was impossible for them to put themselves in the listener's shoes to realize what the experience would be without the context they had.

The metaphor here for the Curse of Knowledge is revisionist history. We often skip the nitty-gritty of history, assuming away the difficulties inherent in getting to the often-tidy conclusion of major events. The Curse of Knowledge prevents us as experts from fully appreciating the effort we made to get to the first steps of our expertise, and we tell others and ourselves a different story, which can be frustrating to those at the beginning steps of this journey.

The Curse of Knowledge during Opportunity Identification

The Opportunity Identification phase is a critical place to be aware that your knowledge may be holding you back, by limiting your ability to see your customer needs. You know a lot more about your business than your customers will ever know, such as how it works, why you do things the way you do, and what can or cannot be done in the current circumstances. They don't care why customer service can't solve their problem. They only care about getting their problem solved.

A financial services project we facilitated several years ago provides one example. The client team experienced a huge aha moment during an opportunity exploration session with consumers who were generating "broad wishes" for what would delight them if offered by their bank. One consumer observed that, while she understood that the bank would use the money in her savings account to make money by investing or loaning it out, she wished she could have a say in how it was used, so that it was used for purposes she could agree with. The clients and the Ideas To Go team were in the back room listening to this discussion. When this comment got lots of violent nodding in agreement from the other consumers, one of the client team members exclaimed, "*Oh my gosh*! They actually think it's their money!"

Why would this be astonishing? Of course consumers think it's their money. That's how most of us think about our money when it's in the bank. It seems like an almost laughable, all-too-obvious statement, but, to the Ideas To Go team's great surprise, none of the clients were laughing when this exclamation came out. They were all nodding and agreeing that this was a revelation to them. This was the Curse of Knowledge at play. They all knew so much about how a bank runs, and how a bank pools all the deposited money so that no individual dollar is really tied to an individual person, that it would never occur to them that the customers would think they should have a say in how "their" part of that pooled money was used.

And the explicit knowledge we all have is only part of the knowledge gap. Think about how much *tacit* knowledge you have about your business from the thousands of observations, impressions, and snippets of passing conversations in your environment at work that you have absorbed without recognizing that it might be teachable or conveyable knowledge.

This is the danger we all risk. We simply cannot put ourselves into our customers' shoes. We can't. Most of us think we can, and we regularly try. We speculate about what our customers want and need, but we must remember that it is only speculation. If we fall into the trap of thinking we absolutely understand them and thus know what they need and prefer, we are potentially missing out on huge areas of opportunity that might unlock the next big change in our industry. We need to remain humble and open, and by doing that, get the right customer input at the right time in our innovation work.

The obvious way to mitigate this bias during the Opportunity Discovery phase is to talk to customers. Ask them lots of questions. And don't ask them yes/no questions, or "would you prefer this or that" questions. These questions limit what you might discover to what *you* have identified as potential opportunity areas. You need to prompt the customers to talk about their needs in a way that will open the door to new potential opportunity areas that you haven't even thought of (with that Curse of Knowledge you're carrying with you all the time). Open-ended questions about what they wish for, or what their life is like, will open the door to new understanding for you.

Whenever possible, ask the customers to do some preparation work before you talk to them. We do this for every innovation project we design. This gives people time to really think about their lives and their needs more deeply than if they have to respond in the moment to questions they weren't prepared for—and probably haven't been thinking about. And the questions you ask should have some creative edge. Don't ask just the obvious questions, because you'll get only obvious answers that have already been discovered. Ask different questions that require new thinking. Some examples of the types of preparation questions we frequently use with our *Creative Consumers*® associates include:

- If you could create the ideal version of _____ (whatever the category of product or service is), assuming you were starting from scratch and none of the current rules apply, what would it be like?
- Write a song, poem, or short story about X (the aspect of your life related to our topic).

With questions such as these, you will get amazing results. We've had people perform soliloquies, sing a song to a backbeat they played on their cell phones, and create a video about their morning showering routine. You'll get dramatically deeper insights into the lives and needs of your customers when you ask them to actually illustrate them for you in a richer way.

For the best results, work with creatively bold customers. By "creatively bold" we mean people who are comfortable with not appearing smarter or more virtuous than they are. They have enough sense of self to admit the truth about what they do, say, or believe that wouldn't necessarily paint them in the best light. You may have had the experience in qualitative research when you can tell the people participating are hedging, probably subconsciously, in the service of self-protection.

This happens even though they know they're unlikely to see the other people in the room ever again. It isn't rational, but it's certainly human.

For example, you will probably never hear any mom admit she buys sugary cereal for her kids. If you only listened to what the majority says, you would assume that no one ever buys it. Yet millions of dollars of it are sold every year. You're looking for those customers who readily admit they buy it, and perhaps even eat it themselves. In the opportunity exploration phase, these people are going to be more helpful in unlocking new insights and opportunities. Don't worry too much about having a representative sample of the target audience at this stage. You're driving to *possibilities* here, which matter more than involving the projectable sample of customers later in the process to evaluate, and which will include more than the creatively bold. Find people who naturally display the ability of give-and-take—they're fine agreeing with others when that occurs organically, but they don't need for that to happen in order to participate actively. The very nature of upfront work is to find more ideas to consider, not to find *the answer*.

The Challenge of Working with Customers in Innovation

We don't deny it. Working with customers in innovation can be challenging. After thirty-five years of customer-centered innovation, we can tell you that it makes a difference which customers you talk to. Most people are very literal and grounded in their current experience. However, there is also a small percentage of the population that think laterally. While it isn't exactly the opposite of literal thinking, "lateral thinking"[1] allows people to see things as they could be, not just as they are. It also gives people the ability to apply analogies and metaphors to something that has not yet been fully defined, to give it context and help shape solutions that might not have been identified had the person just looked at it from the point of "this is all it is."

Here's a quick breakdown of what we mean:

Literal-thinking traditional consumers are good at looking at a product that currently exists and telling you what they like about it. And they are very good at telling you what they *don't* like about it. However, they struggle with:

- Products that are so far out that they can't imagine them in their current day-to-day life.

- Products that have a usage context different from a currently existing product; for example, a new way to brush your teeth.

- Products that don't have a benefit that fills a need they currently have; for example, the iPod before it was introduced.

Lateral-thinking customers are possibility seers and natural problem solvers. These thinkers are the basis of both our *Creative Consumers* associates and iCoN® panelists. Both of these groups of consumers that we use in Ideation are identified by their inherent problem-solving capabilities, and then trained in Ideation and more extensive lateral-thinking techniques. These unique individuals give our clients the ability to ask those curiosity questions we mentioned before, such as "what's next?" and "what's missing?" They also help marketers and market researchers with challenges that traditional consumers can't tackle, such as:

- Bringing a product to life once a concept comes back from quantitative testing—including product, packaging, and usage experience.

- Imagining future line extensions, and even next-generation possibilities by looking at existing lines.

The Curse of Knowledge in Ideation

The whole idea here is to try to recapture a little consumer naïveté and naturalism. Don't settle for insights that are really reverse benefits in disguise. Benefit articulations that take for granted your brand's or product's obvious superiority won't get you there. Support/Reason To Believe language that requires some baseline category knowledge might not be the best move (with some allowance for categories where customers are especially sensitive to patronization, such as corporate IT and vinyl-record geekery!).

Time to blast away layers of presupposed knowledge and (un)awareness. Time to surface and then challenge embedded assumptions. Time for "Assumption Busting."

Assumption Busting is a simple tool that puts a searing spotlight on the "no-duhs" of your offerings to see what we might be able to bust loose.

Imagine for a moment that your challenge is to think of new ideas for salad dressing. Try to come up with a few right now—don't skip ahead!

What kinds of ideas did you come up with? At this point, we often hear things like chocolate salad dressing, or meat-flavored salad dressing, or salad dressings inspired by your favorite cocktails. All really interesting ideas, *if* you are looking for ideas that don't challenge the basic nature of salad dressing or the way it's currently manufactured, packaged, or sold. These ideas are all simply variations of the same kind of dressing that already exists.

The Curse of Knowledge causes us to rely on past experience to shortcut problem solving, so we don't have to spend time "learning" things we already know in order to solve a new problem. While this style of thinking is more efficient from a System 1 perspective, it is hardly innovative. We instantly, and subconsciously, call on everything we know from the past to come up with solutions. While this ability to call on past learning is an incredibly useful trait in many situations (it's one of the reasons humans are at the top of the food chain), when you're looking for new ideas, it actually becomes a significant barrier.

The minute you see the words "salad dressing," your brain calls on all your past experience and knowledge of salad dressing and makes a bunch of instantaneous assumptions that you're likely not aware of. This limits the range of ideas you might come up with. These assumptions are probably things like:

- It comes in a bottle.

- It's liquid.

- It's refrigerated/cold.

- You put it on lettuce

- You serve the salad in a bowl or plate.

- You eat the salad with a fork.

Using the salad dressing challenge again, assume one of the above "facts" is *not* true. What ideas could you come up with then? You might think of ideas like:

- Salad dressing that you heat in the microwave (if it's not cold).

- Dressing for fruit, or for meat (if you don't put it on lettuce).

- Powder whose full flavor is activated when it contacts the moisture of the lettuce (if it's not liquid).

- Salad dressing in the form of a wrap, like fruit leather, so you can eat the salad on the go (if you don't serve it on a plate).

- Salad dressing in the form of a skewer onto which you slide the lettuce and vegetables, so you can enjoy it one-handed (if you don't eat it with a fork).

As you can see, the nature of the ideas that arise after busting our embedded assumptions is dramatically different from the ideas that came before. That's because you're not limiting your creativity with any unconscious guardrails.

Using deliberate tools like Assumption Busting can help you consciously surface and challenge your hidden assumptions. To help surface your assumptions about your own business, generate a long list of statements that start with things like:

- Well, in our business everyone knows . . .

- We have to . . .

- Our product is/does/has . . .

- Well, of course we . . .

- We make/sell . . .

- We do X by Y . . .

Then, take one assumption at a time, and say, "What if that's not true?" What ideas can you think of now?

When you do this, be sure you're tackling an assumption that's within the scope of your challenge or your project. You don't want to spend time busting assumptions or "pet peeves" about conditions that are clearly beyond the scope of your control. For example, we do a lot of work with pharmaceutical companies. One of the assumptions that typically comes up for them is "We're highly regulated." Yes. That's definitely true. And it may not be in the scope of our project to try to change federal regulations. So, once you've generated your list of assumptions, be judicious about which ones you choose to work on to challenge.

Now, time to kick things into high gear. How about some "high-test" Curse of Knowledge–obliterating formula?

Reverse Claimstorming® flips the script on our *Claimstorming®* services by putting *Creative Consumers* associates in the role of the tech expert and allowing them to give a briefing of a new technology back to your team. Whenever we work with clients on new product possibilities based on a new technology (e.g., new toothpaste action when it comes in contact with your mouth, or the different way a new OTC medication works to reduce the burden of symptoms), we ask for one of *their* R&D experts to break the tech down into terms that the *Creative Consumers* will understand, and then allow the consumers to collect "Nagging Questions" about it. These questions are helpful to point to opportunities to tell the story better, more simply, more compellingly, etc.

Reverse Claimstorming allows us to check how much the Curse of Knowledge might be getting in the way. After being exposed to the technology and doing some initial Ideation, we come back a little later to have the consumers role-play as the R&D experts. This helps the client in two really important ways: (1) It will clarify whether the consumer is really *getting it* and (2) Hearing it in the consumers' own words will start driving the client further in the direction of Relevance and much better consumer naturalism.

In one successful campaign, the Heath Brothers tee up the concern for consumer naturalism nicely, playing with other ways President Kennedy might have communicated the early-1960s national mission to "put a man on the moon and return him safely by the end of the decade":

Had John F. Kennedy been a CEO, he would have said, "Our mission is to become the international leader in the space industry through maximum team-centered innovation and strategically targeted aerospace initiatives." Fortunately, JFK was more intuitive than a modern-day CEO; he knew that opaque, abstract missions don't captivate and inspire people. The moon mission was a classic case of a communicator's dodging the Curse of Knowledge. It was a brilliant and beautiful idea—a single idea that motivated the actions of millions of people for a decade.[2]

Goodness gracious. Can you play "Corporate Buzzword Bingo" with it? You're likely tripping over the Curse of Knowledge. Keep it simple, keep it consumer-real.

The Curse of Knowledge in the Development Phase

The blindness caused by the Curse of Knowledge is also potentially dangerous in the Development Phase. As ideas are developed and refined, it is all too easy to fall prey to the Curse of Knowledge and decide on things that make perfect sense to us, but might not make any sense at all to customers.

This isn't just about tradeoff of features or usability—it applies to communicating our new offering as well. "It's not like there's a powerful constituency for overcomplicated, lifeless prose" as one presenter on this topic noted.[3] We want to make our innovations transparent and intuitive, so we need to be extra vigilant when we start pulling together the full proposition.

The assumptions we make—whether consciously or not—can trip us up. The more expert we are, the more these embedded assumptions limit our thinking. The more experience we have in a subject, the more existing assumptions we have about it. We are likely not even aware of all the embedded assumptions we have. Many of them are so ingrained in our thinking that it wouldn't even occur to us to question them. They are presumed to be fact, if we are even conscious of them at all. So in an area where you have lots of experience and expertise, for example, in your job, you have lots of these limiting assumptions. You don't realize it, but you have them. We all do.

This means we need lots of check-ins during the development phase. Otherwise, we run the risk of making decisions about the product, or customer service, or pricing, or packaging that make complete sense to us, but seem like complete nonsense to a customer. This is why it is so essential to continue to get customer input and feedback throughout the development phase. Longitudinal consumer involvement is what we recommend to our clients; we suggest they check in with customers after Ideation and then again once a product or service is fully developed. These recurring consumer checks make it almost certain that decisions made along the development cycle still make sense and are still relevant, and that the product or service is still buy-worthy to customers.

Consumer involvement requires curiosity. The best marketers we've worked with do not assume they know their customers to the nth degree. Their curiosity keeps their Curse of Knowledge at bay with key questions like:

- What is changing now that _____ is happening in the marketplace?

- Why are our customers doing what they are doing?

- What else do they need?

- How do they feel about this change we have made?

- What is the underlying need that is driving this new trend?

- How do they like to be talked to about this?

Too often marketers use past research as a crutch rather than a spark for new insights. It's far better to turn that prior knowledge into a spur toward new and better value for their customers.

Research is sometimes only relevant for a limited time and only as good as the purpose and scope of the particular study. Saying that you *know* something based on past research can be like saying that you know exactly what Antarctica is like because you saw a glacier from the deck of your Alaskan cruise in 2009. Different circumstances, different time, different context—and therefore, different learning.

Once you're aware of the Curse of Knowledge, it is easier to access what might be influencing your decisions, what your inherent assumptions are, and what you might do to overcome it.

5

Status Quo Bias—
The Bird in the Hand

"In times of change, learners inherit the earth,
while the learned find themselves beautifully equipped
to deal with a world that no longer exists."

—Eric Hoffer

THE STATUS QUO BIAS. ALSO KNOWN AS *CHANGE IS BAD, SAME IS*
good. It's in our nature as humans to nonconsciously believe that whatever
situation currently exists is better than what doesn't exist, reiterating the
loss aversion we discussed in chapter two on Negativity Bias, here specifically in the form of perhaps overvaluing what we have compared to what
we could create.

Status Quo Bias may be one of the greatest effort-savers our species
has developed. Consider the infinite number of life-changing innovations that will never get beyond the imagination of the dreamers—and

weep. *Not doing something* is the omnipresent option, always ready to assert its attractiveness.

As discussed earlier, we default to treating threats as a much bigger deal than opportunities. Doing something new may bring its share of opportunities, but we know for sure that doing so has plenty of threats, even as we acknowledge that we view the supposed threats through the distorting lens of our evolutionary wiring.

Status Quo Bias takes justifiable, seemingly responsible loss-aversion fears and adds the following twists:

- **The Endowment Effect.** We value the "bird in hand" much more highly than a potentially greater payoff we don't yet have, but might get with some probability. (Note: But what if the bird in the hand has avian flu?)

- **Easing Our Entry into the New.** Beyond what we personally possess, we will prefer what is stated by someone else as the status quo in an area that is entirely new to us. We gain comfort from others' reports of the status quo, such as a salesperson telling us that a given color is the go-to color for a class of car we've never owned before. When we're unsure, we're likely to go with the "safe choice" made by the informed crowd, even if there is no objective support for that being an obviously better decision.

- **Collateral Costs.** Some part of us will always be aware of the costs of just doing something new, apart from any direct purchase costs, such as dealing with a new seller, needing to be vigilant until we're sure we can trust him/her, having to go through all the paperwork, etc.

The Status Quo is great as long as the conditions under which it was established remain unchanged. Unfortunately, that's hardly ever the case. The status quo leaks Relevance over time. And something once considered to be unique is only fleetingly so if we're not constantly building upon it. If you are starting to feel comfortable, you're probably already behind.

"It won't happen to us," said the newspaper publishers years before a late-night comedy show became the preferred source of news for an entire generation. A comedy show? Unimaginable.

"It won't happen to us," said record labels right before a group of college kids invented file sharing. How could they have anticipated that something illegal was going to do them in? That's just nuts.

"It won't happen to us," thought your authors' favorite retailer of the 90s, Barnes & Noble; after all, they'd just reinvented themselves and created "big-box" bookselling. Weren't they supposed to get a few decades of being the king of the industry out of this? Unforeseeable.

"It won't happen to us," thought mid-2000s Pure Digital Technologies, makers of the Flip® Video Cam—c'mon they just barely came out! Or Garmin and TomTom in the once-booming GPS industry. That makes no sense at all. We just got going!

Unimaginable. Nuts. Unforeseeable. Nonsense.

The bird in the hand just might have avian flu.

Welcome to the new status quo.

One of the stealthiest risks in relying on the comforts of the status quo is the risk of omission. It's that willingness to accept the consequences of doing nothing rather than worry about what might happen if you did something. When it comes to innovation, omission literally gets you nowhere. Even though it might appear "safer," it could very well be the wrong decision *and* provide the guilt that you didn't even try to do something. There's little comfort in that. If you take the leap of faith to make a potentially risky decision early enough in development, you can learn more at the right time—rather than learning too late.

Due to the Status Quo Bias, it is often extremely difficult to truly perceive the risks of doing nothing. And if you do see the risks, it can still be all-too-difficult to convince others of those risks. It's pretty easy to quantify the downside of Risks of Commission—when things go wrong we know *what* happened and *whom* to blame, *how* much it all cost, *what* we'll never do again, etc. We have language for this, and as much as we *love* gallows humor, calling after-action reviews "postmortems" may not be the most helpful mindset. Death and blame are fun for a little while, but may not be serving us well as a productive approach to learning.

Play this out within a business culture that too often rewards inaction in the name of being prudent, and throw in the pressures of post hoc market-analyst scrutiny that will still punish Risks of Commission while ignoring those of Omission until it's too late—and hey, look what we've created.

Risks of Omission *are* tricky to quantify; we have few tools for thinking through the impact of what we *didn't* do, while we have an impressive armamentarium of analytical tools to dial in the detail of errors of Commission. But shouldn't we at least acknowledge that risks of inaction have their costs? And that those costs often have a more detrimental effect on a company than those of their quantifiable-risk siblings?

Although impossible to calculate at the individual-project level, the accumulation of "paths not taken" is ultimately what takes many companies down, often more so than the total errors of commission. Let's talk about what was, sadly, the Kodak Moment for the post-2010 period: Kodak had at least a twenty-five-year heads-up on digital photography and did not do nearly enough to translate their leadership in silver-halide photography to winning in digital. *Winning?* Kodak didn't even place or ultimately show. Kodak had advantages that most other companies didn't, including the strongest top-of-mind consumer associations that *Kodak* meant *photography*, and the deep emotional resonance that *Kodak Moments* were precisely the ones that we all cherish most. The drug of unimaginable success for 111 years lulled Kodak into inaction, and Risks of Omission took it out. What a sad example of "*The Innovator's Dilemma*." Clearly, Risks of Omission are also key operands in the fate equations of Research in Motion, Nokia, AOL, Gateway Computer, and MySpace (to name just a few).

So then, why are we ignoring Risks of Omission? The difficulty in quantifying them shouldn't result in not accounting for them at all. Being precisely wrong in ignoring Risks of Omission seems so much more attractive or important than being vaguely right were we to take baby steps in factoring in these hard-to-quantify risks. The ability to capture the detail of Risks of Commission shouldn't give them the only place in the risk discussion. Can we start moving a little beyond a ratio of 100:0 Commission to Omission and get to something that looks at least a little like 70:30? Can we make sure we talk about the deadliness of inaction before we're satisfied that the risk analysis is complete?

One of our colleagues had the experience on a work team dealing with balancing the downside risk of diluting the brand by entering into the kids' market vs. the upside opportunity of profiting from that market.

I spent some time at Quaker Oats, working on the Gatorade business. (Gatorade is now managed out of the Pepsi division, but at the time I was there, it was in the Quaker division.) We had identified a potential opportunity to sell Gatorade in juice boxes to kids. The project team was strongly advocating developing this product, but we were not being successful selling this idea to senior management. They were very resistant to marketing Gatorade to kids; their viewpoint at the time was that it was only for adults, and particularly for "heavy sweat" situations. We had meeting after meeting where we presented opportunities for Gatorade, and this particular opportunity kept getting pushed to the bottom of the list. In hindsight, I now know this was due to Status Quo Bias—they couldn't see past the current situation to imagine that a new situation might be better. So the project was essentially shelved, although the project team sort of kept it moving forward on the sly, albeit very slowly, since we didn't have any official resources committed to it.

About six months after the project was shelved, we received some news from one of our salespeople—he had seen launch materials in a buyer's office that showed the Kool-Aid brand was launching a juice-box beverage, positioned as a sports drink for kids. Suddenly, everything changed. This news, and the pictures we got of the actual product that was about to be launched by Kool-Aid, had managed to break through the Status Quo Bias and allow people to see that a new reality was definitely coming. And in this case, a new reality in which a competitive brand might end up "owning" the kids' sports drink market would clearly be worse than the current reality.

Since we had kept the project moving a little bit, once we got the go-ahead, we were able to fast-track the product and we actually managed to get to market before the competitive launch. The product turned out to be a huge success—one of the most successful line extensions the brand had ever experienced.

The metaphor to keep in mind about Status Quo Bias is balloon ballast. Visualize the sandbags in the carriage underneath a huge hot-air balloon. The bags are there deliberately to keep the balloon on the ground. We have no chance of gaining any altitude worth the effort if we don't bail on the ballast. The perspective gained when we view our area from an inspiring altitude is indispensable.

Status Quo Bias in Opportunity Identification

Facing risk is, well, risky. Work teams regularly examine new possibilities with a scrutiny *never* applied to what they're currently doing—especially in Opportunity ID. It seems once you start down a path, the evaluation of it has already been completed, never to be reconsidered. When you're considering *only* the risks of the new, the "new" seems pretty risky.

A smarter approach to identifying opportunities would be to simply add the status quo to the list of options you could take. Then you're not assuming away the obviousness of the case for it, but checking to see if the things that hold up to current needs can also promise ongoing vitality for your business versus the new, unchartered opportunities that could take your brand in a new direction. Use the same criteria to assess new possibilities, such as the following:

- The Big Two: Potential to establish Uniqueness and to address a Relevant customer need.

- Fit with brand equity.

- Addressing the needs of a big-enough customer base and not just an impassioned niche within it.

- Some heuristic about "shelf life of the option" should be in the mix as well, as we know how Uniqueness and Relevance leak over time, and this criterion alone might make us assess the status quo more effectively.

Also, when it comes to the status quo, be very aware of entrenched internal interests. Current approaches may have been the brain-baby years ago of someone far up the current chain of command. No strategy or operational playbook should be considered evergreen: even the clearest-eyed management type is human and has messy, intertwined emotions attached to those earlier decisions. In a nonthreatening way, you must address what came before you and take these folks into account. You need to get them on board—at least enough not to be an ongoing source of friction.

Status Quo Bias in Ideation

As we start pinning down Target Areas for Ideation and get into specific possibilities, a great way to engage people and help them let go of their natural Status Quo Bias is to reward them (with laughs, group admiration, perhaps a toy to the top performer) to come up with extreme ideas. This exercise lets people have some fun with letting go of the current situation, which makes it a little easier.

Get Fired, Get Hired. This is an innovative technique that is both fun and *very* productive. It consistently produces new and different ideas. Not only does it generate ideas in totally new areas, it also adds energy and momentum for solving the problem.

The objective is to really stretch thinking—in this case, stretch it so far that the idea might just get you fired if you actually executed it. These "get fired" ideas must actually solve the problem you're working on, but they can be illegal, immoral, impossible, ridiculous, or even ridiculously expensive. Or some delightfully wrong combination of the above. The mistake you'll make is being too polite with this initial stimulus—really push it. We need the energy of "the new" that we can only get by radically violating the current rules.

1. Start by writing down one Get Fired idea.

2. Exchange your idea with someone else.

3. Use the Get Fired idea to spark Get Hired ideas by doing any of the following:

   • Keep the idea relatively the same but do less (or more) of it.

   • Find an interesting word or phrase in the idea and constructively build on it.

   • Do the opposite of what is written down.

   • Find the underlying principle in the idea and apply that principle to your challenge.

   • Do a *Forness* response on the idea and use either side to spark new ideas.

The goal is to keep some of the transgressive energy from the Get Fired idea moving forward—push to some *solution* without out-and-out *dilution*. Get Hired ideas will hit the sweet spot of Uniqueness and Relevance that we're always targeting.

Deprivation. Here's one way to blast past the status quo—come right out and ban some part of it. For example, if you were trying to come up with new communications possibilities for a breakthrough sports drink, you might ask the group to list category clichés (verbal and visual) on a chart and then ban those from the possibilities we'd generate. Take away most or all of the following:

• Quenching

• Replenishing

• Refreshing

- Electrolytes

- Hydration

- Recovery

- Splashing imagery, particularly slo-mo

- Allusions to competitive edge

Hey, we understand—there are certain category costs of entry that have to be addressed. This is going to be tough. But fun. Bring the category stuff back in later, once you've developed completely fresh territory that establishes an entirely new context for the reassurance language. Don't lead with category expectations.

Where could that take you? What might be several completely new narratives for sports drinks? Wouldn't it be "refreshing" to come up with a new way to talk to your target? Try going to a higher-order benefit space or making a lateral move to an adjacent benefit space. Try a very different voice and see where that might take you. "Electrolytes" banned? Cool—go even harder into the science, where "electrolytes" is too soft a consumer-y term for those who really know what's going on at a much deeper level. Then ladder up from there to see what new emotional territory you can lock down.

Goals for Ideation. Let's apply some brute-force power to shatter the status quo. How about starting early in the process with some metrics to raise the stakes? Given that the cost of an error early on can run 100 to 100,000 times less than it does later, why not spend a little more time and money on things like the following:

- **Broad Opportunity Areas Considered.** Triple this early on so you can be even choosier about where you focus Ideation and the creation of specific product possibilities. Make sure that half the Broad Opportunity Areas are defined differently from the way anyone else in your industry would define them—don't merely go for the obvious. Pushing yourself here gives you a great start on distinctive competitive advantage.

- **Total Number of Product Possibilities Generated.** Double the number of possibilities compared to your last high-water mark. The next time after that, add another 50 percent just to see where it takes you. Give yourself many more possibilities than you had before so you can set an even higher bar on what moves forward. As the saying goes, "More is different," not just more. When you factor up, you get a sense of freedom, and the pressure for any one idea to be "the winner" quickly diminishes. You start to understand that the task here is to combine and synthesize, not find ideas that sprout fully formed from a god's forehead—that way madness lies. Getting great grist for the mill is what you want here. The grinding is still to come, and it's gratifying.

- **Total Number of 'Big Ideas' or 'Proto-Concepts.'** Again, shoot for at least doubling the number of starter areas for Concept Development. Take up to a lavish ten minutes on each, pulling together a rough product description, compelling customer insight or need, benefit articulation, etc. Do all this before starting in on Concept Development. Don't make these too pretty too early—just get them half-baked and get a lot more of them to this stage. Let the specter of prematurely settling for "The Answer" haunt and bother you. Try much more stuff here.

This is where spending a little more time and money pays off. Slow down here to hurry up through the rest of the New Product Development process. Raising the bar in Ideation is a great way to stave off the seductive pull of the status quo.

There's another status-quo-smashing opportunity here beyond the specifics of the one initiative you're working on at that moment. It helps to approach every Ideation phase with both a clear picture of what the specific project needs *and* a vision of growth for the process itself. Use each Ideation session as an opportunity to get better at that part of the process. Build in an ongoing expectation of raising your Ideation-process game, and you build adaptive capability for the long run as you get the great results for the immediate needs.

Status Quo Bias in Concept Development

The Status Quo Bias can also turn up in Concept Development and Testing in an interesting way. In Ideation, even the most risk-averse can offer up ideas—because they are just ideas, and even wild ideas can help get to better places. But when it comes to actually committing to an idea and turning it into a fully formed concept, our tendency is to immediately regress to being practical and throwing away the "weird" stuff. This is often a place of team tension, because the people who make a point of asking for creative ideas will often be the first to reject them. The resulting attitude of those people tasked with coming up with all the new ideas can too often be, "Why did we even bother trying?"

Implicit-association-test research[1] shows that decision makers of all stripes—business leaders, scientific institutions, etc.—support creativity in the ranks as a stated goal and then regularly turn down the very thing they're ostensibly requesting. Even teachers have been shown to dislike students who show the curiosity and creativity that is acknowledged as important for their students to develop.

So why does the pursuit of creative ideas get thwarted, even when requested? According to the research, like other deep-rooted human biases, there is an innate bias against creativity. We have an innate bias against creativity, which goes hand in hand with the Status Quo Bias. Creative ideas are by definition novel, paradigm-shifting ideas that undermine the existing order. And we feel a strong urge to protect the existing order, due to the Status Quo Bias. The easiest path to take is to reject it and inadvertently stick with the status quo.

In innovation, the ideal we're pursuing is Uniqueness and Relevance. Uniqueness is the more obvious sign of creativity, but it sets up a clash because of concerns about Relevance for customers and because it is perceived as risky, since it is a departure from the status quo. Uniqueness and practicality are often seen as inversely related. But higher Uniqueness is actually closely connected to higher Relevance.

New markets are created when Uniqueness and Relevance come together. Introduced as a consumer offering within the past twenty-five years, the "grabber" pickup tool was big news for assistive technology. Many simple tasks unavailable to elderly consumers and those otherwise afflicted with limited joint mobility became doable again, increasing this customer's sense of self-sufficiency. However, given low technical barriers to entry, "me-too" offerings too quickly came in, commoditizing the category. We looked up the number of brands of grabbers on Amazon.com, and counted sixty-two different ones—and that was only on the first six pages of our search. The fact that there are so many of them probably speaks to their Relevance—they're useful tools, so lots of companies make them. However, the ones we saw all have virtually the same features—the only significant difference was that a few of them could fold for easier storage. And that lack of Uniqueness matters. Not one of those grabbers had a brand name that any of us had ever heard of. It's probably reasonable to assume that they're not huge sellers for the companies who make them, even though they might still be relevant now;

but they're like salt—an important commodity. Relevance has degrees to it—from the "Man, I love how this makes my life easier" recognition every time you use the product to the dissatisfaction you feel when a staple of your routine goes missing. Both Uniqueness and Relevance "leak" over time.

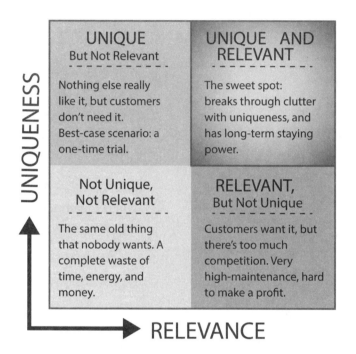

In order to get to greater Relevance, we have to go out there on Uniqueness. But risk increases with Uniqueness—so we get both greater hits and misses for Relevance. We're talking potential failure, social rejection (from peers and powers-that-be), and uncertainties around costs and the length of time to bring something really new to market. Part of what makes innovation so tricky is that we have to contend with the double bind of conflicting social pressures to support innovation and never making a mistake.

Here are some ways to escape the tug of Status Quo Bias when developing concepts:

- **Remember the risk of the status quo itself.** Again, consider that the greater risk just might be the risk of omission. What will you forego if you don't test propositions that go further out than the more conservative comfort concerns allow? Remember that the status quo has risks of its own that are often underestimated.

- **Get the learning.** Often the fears of disaster aren't supported by your customers. Talk to them. You're not commissioning new asset bases yet, just trying to get knowledge that the competition doesn't have.

- **Avoid the soon-to-be commoditized.** Ask yourself how many of the concepts you're developing might be similar to what the competition would go after. Land on the percentage that fits your business needs, but if that percentage is high, be ready to be really cheap if you're not going to be Unique.

- **Specific issues vs. vague unease.** Convert the vague unease regarding possible directions into meaningful issues to tackle. Problems are just jobs. Break it down. Let your customers clarify the issues instead deciding for them. In trickier cases after conducting research with target respondents, a trained, more articulate panel of creative problem-solvers can help identify and solve for potential risks before you kill a concept completely. Remember, solve for Uniqueness first and then beef up the Relevance. Don't be too quick to give up on a really interesting concept—it might be tricky precisely because no competitor has gone anywhere around there yet, and some ambiguity in customer response is natural.

- **Get ready to go to work on Uniqueness.** Afterward, should you be lucky enough to find that your test respondents have some real interest in some propositions that will be a challenge to bring to market, be ready to break down that challenge into pieces that can be tackled in short learning cycles. What can the team resolve in two days? Four? Ten at the most?

Status Quo Bias in Concept Testing

The status quo is often why it can be difficult to get helpful feedback from customers on a not-fully-developed idea or product. Most "traditional" consumers assume that current (existing) solutions are probably better than something that doesn't yet exist. Coupled with Negativity Bias, the Status Quo Bias makes it difficult for the average customer to trust that something outside their current understanding is better for them. Give credit to Henry Ford. If he listened to what people wanted, he would have bred a faster horse—and let go of his idea of a better way to get around.

It is so important in Concept Testing to think critically of the data you are collecting. Before you throw away an idea based on concept testing, think about how you can optimize it.

The DREAM™ technique is a great way to get past tried-and-true thinking—to really push toward optimization or even complete newness. DREAM stands for Delete-Reduce-Enhance-Add-Maintain. By walking yourself through this exercise on any number of facets of your business—or perceived facets of your business, you almost ensure you are breaking away from the status quo.

Take the circus for example. Cirque du Soleil helped redefine what "circus" means by reinventing it. We are not saying they used this model, but if they did, it might have looked like this:

- Delete large animal acts.

- Reduce the kid focus.

- Enhance the adult appeal.

- Add storylines.

- Maintain the spectacle, fun, and wonderment.

Just by walking through this exercise, you can see it opens up new target audience possibilities, new venue options, and new revenue streams. One of the best benefits of DREAM is that it can be applied anywhere in the development cycle. Even as late as launch: Can you delete coupons? Reduce TV? Enhance the buying experience? Add a sense of community? Maintain the quality that is expected from your brand?

If an idea keeps coming up and your response is, "We thought of that before," you should change that to ask yourself, "Why haven't we made this happen?"

ONE OF THE BEST BOOKS ON INNOVATION FROM THE AUGHTS, 2000–2009, is a little stealthy—most people think it's about baseball, but baseball is just the context to provide the thrilling real story of creating entirely new, proprietary knowledge.

The idea behind *Moneyball* is that the conventional wisdom within baseball through the 1990s was subjective and regularly wrong. The received wisdom of baseball's elders worked until

Oakland figured out how to create something that worked notice-ably better. The stats that all MLB teams used to assess talent were those that were easiest to collect years ago, when the sophistica-tion of computer processing and decision theory didn't intersect with the then-best thinking in baseball. The story shows how the Oakland front office took advantage of better analysis of player per-formance to assemble a team based on smarter prediction of the factors that created success.

Through the zero-based rethinking about the most important stats, on-base percentage and slugging percentage were found to be much stronger predictors of offensive success, and since no one else valued these attributes, they were inexpensive to acquire, leav-ing the more-traditionally minded front offices regularly scratching their heads with Oakland trades that made little sense within the established way of valuing talent.

Entirely new, proprietary knowledge leads to actions that con-fuse those playing the old game. Fun.

With this new approach, Oakland was competitive with a player salary pool of $44 million in salary, while big-market teams spent multiples of that—the Yankees spent over $125 million in payroll that same season. With the smaller fan base, and hence revenues from those fans, Oakland had to reduce big pockets for salary as a competitive edge. A knowledge edge made up the difference. Oak-land went to the playoffs in 2002 and 2003.

Moneyball plays out the need to keep the knowledge advantage; as other teams started aping Oakland's approach, cutting into the effectiveness of this new approach, Oakland had to turn the light on other parts of the game that hadn't been rethought, such as what truly worked on defense.

The advantages of proprietary knowledge are increasingly short-lived. The model of companies as fortresses guarding proprietary IP stocks is outdated, as those stocks' values are quickly outdone by the knowledge stocks of competitors. Today, knowledge *flows* matter more than knowledge *stocks*,[2] and creating "pull platforms" that attract knowledge flows is a better strategy for most businesses than the expensive building and maintaining the equivalent of the Wall along the northern border of the Seven Kingdoms. Smart IP protection is still necessary, it just needs to be redirected to enable flows, not protect stocks.

6

Confabulation—Of Course That's Why I Did That!

"When I was a kid, I spent a lot of time in the desert of
Southern California—out in the desert scrub and dry bunchgrass,
surrounded by . . . coyotes and rattlesnakes. The reason I am
still here today is because I have nonconscious
processes that were honed by evolution."[1]

—Michael S. Gazzaniga

OUR NONCONSCIOUS PROCESSES ARE DRIVING OUR BUS MUCH MORE than we want to acknowledge.

It's October 17, 2002, on a train platform in the sweltering heat of India. A man named David MacLean wakes up, standing, with no idea who he is or why he is there. A tourist policeman sees him, disheveled and confused, sizes up the most likely scenario, and tells MacLean that he's a drug addict—since that is usually what's going on with most of the Americans who look and act this way in that area. MacLean actually feels relieved to know this, to have something to hold onto. And it makes sense, given his condition. Within minutes, MacLean's mind starts supplying him images, memories, song lyrics, and other sense impressions of his drug-addict lifestyle. He even remembers a red-haired woman named Christina as his doping-up companion. He later sees an abandoned building that he's convinced is his flophouse. It's all starting to come back to him.

The problem? It was all made up. And yet it all seemed so real to him.

How did this happen? Fleeting sense memories were pressed into service by his brain to help build this new identity. The image of Christina may have come from a TV documentary he once saw. The image of the flophouse could have been triggered by a run-down building in his peripheral vision that he subconsciously registered as a plausible drug den in India.

What had actually happened was that MacLean's form of amnesia was the result of a commonly used malarial medication he had been taking. He was, in fact, in India on a fellowship from the US government.[2]

What's going on here?

The plot thickens. Confabulation is an automatic tendency that we all experience to tell a coherent story about the rationale for our behavior. This tendency is deeply ingrained and irresistible, and the interpretation comes to us effortlessly, so that we fully believe the story is true. We confabulate all the time without realizing that, in fact, our behavior was driven by a complex set of nonconscious processes we do not have access to. Our beliefs about our motives, which seem so true and reasonable, are actually not the true reasons for our behavior.

Gazzaniga elaborates:

When we set out to explain our actions, they are all post-hoc explanations using post-hoc observations with no access to nonconscious processing. Not only that, but our left brain also fudges things a bit to fit into a makes-sense story. It is only when the stories stray too far from the facts that the right brain pulls the reins in. These explanations are all based on what makes it into our consciousness, but the reality is the actions and the feelings happen before we are consciously aware of them—and most of them are the results of nonconscious processes, which will never make it into the explanations. The reality is, listening to people's explanations of their actions is interesting—and in the case of politicians, entertaining—but often a waste of time.[3]

While confabulation can occur as a result of some medical condition, or as a reaction to a medication, we all resort to confabulation, daily. We can't avoid it. We regularly find post-hoc rationalizations for our behavior, which is mostly driven by our nonconscious. Further, these explanations seem totally reasonable to us, and we are unaware that, in fact, they are *not* the reason that we made a particular decision. While confabulation can be even more intensified by a medical condition (in the case of amnesia, where there is nothing else to go on), the healthy brain constantly engages in it. It is an essential process in our brains.

The spate of nonconscious actions and those actions set in motion through the energy-conserving guidance from System 1 ensure that we won't have a bulletproof defense for all our doings. We simply don't have the time or capability to build a perfect case for every action before we take it.

One basic need separating us from other animals is the need for meaning and coherence. We need to make sense of what's going on, even if there's not much inherent sense in a given situation. Confabulation is so natural to us that it can be hard to pinpoint when it's happening. In our innovation work, confabulation tricks us into believing an insight because it was stated with good intentions and confidence. But arriving too quickly at a conclusion before exploring the motives for your feelings or actions means you may not be going deep enough to get at the root. This process is most prevalent in the fuzzier, earlier stages of development, and is all too common in focus-group testing, when we're looking diligently for rationale.

For those of us who need to understand customers' motivations, this is pretty alarming.

Think about a time when you walked into the house after a painful commute and overreacted to something. Immediately after the outburst you were probably asked why you reacted so strongly to something so small. And if that "small" thing was the behavior of your partner who has now confronted you about your own behavior, you will instantly launch into self-defense mode using whatever post-hoc observations you might have available in the moment, and even retrieving examples from the past that are "relevant only in hindsight." Anyone who has ever been in a committed relationship will recognize this painful pattern.

In the heat of the moment, we often resort to confabulation as we put together a rational reconstruction of an emotional event—even if it may not be entirely true. Only later are we able to recognize that we were upset about many other things that may have built up during the day and resorted to defending ourselves using current circumstances when confronted about our behavior. It's not a lie. It sounds quite plausible. We completely believe what we are saying at the time. But it's confabulation.

Our metaphor here is unreliable eyewitnesses under testimony. Even the supposedly "objective" perceptions of an eyewitness are hardly objective. Three different people can observe the same sequence of events at the same time and still report things differently, and swear by their reports. They are not lying; they actually believe what they have seen. It's hard to believe that we can't "believe our own eyes," but a very rich body of research has shown that we can't even trust what we "see." Studies show that two eyewitnesses of a given event often contradict each other. They don't believe they're deliberately distorting the facts. They're usually trying to be helpful. But all perspectives are partial, and some modesty in the truthful claims of any one perspective is helpful. We don't bring an impartial video camera to what we see—we bring our entire being to the occasion, and are incapable of being impartial.

Confabulation in Opportunity ID

In Opportunity Identification, confabulation can prevent us from collecting insights that are deeper and more on point. As a primarily rational, logical process, confabulation can result in very plausible-sounding customer input. When this input is expressed in a nonthreatening or nondisruptive way and matches what we hope is true, we're particularly prone to accepting it. But remember that hasty settling won't necessarily lead you to real or accurate representations of the true flesh-and-blood people who actually compose your market.

Researcher Jonathan Haidt says, "My current interest in confabulation is related to the everyday conflict I observe in the business world between linear, rational, formal processes and nonlinear, informal creative processes, and the tendency for (rational processes') thinking to explain successes very much in terms of its own contributions, even when the success has little to do with them—or even despite them."[4]

We all confabulate to some degree. We can't help it. All parts of our brain are in a steady dialogue that is going on outside of our awareness. We're stimuli-processing machines, tuning out most of the stimuli available to our senses, then processing what seems most helpful to us in telling ourselves and others the story about ourselves and the world around us.

Closer, more intimate relationships allow for more honesty and room for us to "cop to" the less-than-perfect aspects of ourselves; but even these have already been vetted by our brain's ability to rationalize, reason, and reconcile new information with what it's learned before.

So, the task here is not to eliminate confabulation in Opportunity Identification, but to minimize it as much as we can. It should come as no surprise that when we believe that we're objectively reporting something that happened, we're usually offering our interpretation. If "Amy" is scowling and has a red face, we tend to go straight to the obvious conclusion that she's angry. Never mind the fact that she has spent the entire day at the beach and is a little uncomfortable with her new sunburn. Our need for a coherent story often gets in the way of understanding what's actually going on.

Take, for example, something as straightforward as teaching your teenage child how to drive a car with a manual transmission. You have probably gone decades without actually thinking about the specifics of how the clutch, brake, acceleration pedals, and gear shift work together to move the car forward, because this complex sequence of behaviors has been (thankfully) relegated to autopilot muscle memory. There was a time, however, when you devoted significant cognitive vigilance using System 2 to coordinate the complex interplay of both feet, your right hand on the gearshift, hearing and feeling what's going on with the gears, etc. But as the automatic processes of System 1 took over, your conscious mind was able to dramatically simplify the whole experience and free up its precious attention span for more important things, such as answering the cell phone. When it's time to teach your child how to use a manual transmission, your conscious mind shares what it knows, "It's just a one-for-one press and release motion between the clutch and the gas." It all sounds quite plausible until the young driver actually tries to apply your simple instructions, verbatim.

The resulting herky-jerky movement of the vehicle quickly escalates the frustration of everyone in the car (and it's not only the clutch that's overheating). Since your conscious mind is convinced that it knows how to drive a stick shift, you resort to repeating the same instructions, only a little louder, assuming that your child is not paying attention. It's only after you decide to take over the driving, and have your conscious mind attend to what your own "System 1" is doing with the pedals, that you realize that your instructions were all wrong. You painfully discover that your conscious mind didn't remember how to drive a stick shift, and you confabulated the simple and elegant "one-for-one press and release" pas de deux of the two pedals. There's a little clutch-riding in the middle there. The actual motion is much more complicated and takes much more patience to achieve. Without an adequate explanation, your mind simply makes one up, and you believe it. Because it became easy for you, you came to believe it was easy to do.

Another great example is touch typing; while we can find all the right keys, if asked to draw the location of all the letters on a keyboard, most people would not be able to do so explicitly and would be able to reconstruct their locations only by imagining where they would reach in order to type that letter.

There are interesting cases of patients with amnesia who lost their memory and could not form any new explicit memories, and yet could still function (navigate their house, cook a meal, etc.) because they could still build habits/scripts and execute them without awareness and without being able to explain how they knew where to go (since they did not explicitly know the layout of their house and couldn't tell you where the kitchen was), or what to do.

In particular with habitual behaviors such as those above involving "muscle memory," our basal ganglia store scripts that have been repeated many times and are able to execute those scripts nonconsciously without much mental effort. And often we don't consciously "know" and cannot explain how we do the behavior.

Whenever we ask our conscious mind to explain what was observed or achieved through our subconscious System 2 processes, it resorts to confabulation. We like to think of ourselves as rational beings, but we are more often "rationalizing" beings, making up a story after the fact to explain our actions. If the simple act of driving a car can evoke passionate confabulation, imagine the amount of confabulation we engage in when more emotions are involved, when more of our sense of identity and self-worth are at stake, or the really tricky stuff about love, parenting, money, politics, meaning in life, things a person stands for, etc. What stories do we tell ourselves about the important things without even being aware that they're just that—stories?

In Opportunity Identification, we're trying to go in deeply. Great insight work is about getting past the superficialities and confabulations that are bound to control our learning. We should allocate some cognitively costly System 2 resources to the task, understanding that the quality of our efforts downstream from Opportunity ID depend on our diligence here.

There are three things you can do to reduce confabulations: (1) Give the Rationalizing Mind a Break, (2) Create an Environment of Transparent Observation, and (3) Work with the Creatively Bold.

Give the Rationalizing Mind a Break

Michael Gazzaniga introduced the idea of the Interpreter Module in one's mind. Gazzaniga observed what happened with patients who had the corpus callosum—a structure that connects the two hemispheres of the brain—severed, in what came to be called "split brain." The two hemispheres couldn't communicate with each other, resulting in the left hemisphere imputing meaning to what the right had done.

Gazzaniga developed what he called the interpreter theory to explain why people—including split-brain patients—have a unified sense of self and mental life. It grew out of tasks in which he asked a split-brain person to explain in words, which uses the left hemisphere, an action that had been directed to and carried out only by the right one. "The left hemisphere made up a post-hoc answer that fit the situation." In one of Gazzaniga's favorite examples, he flashed the word "smile" to a patient's right hemisphere and the word "face" to the left hemisphere, and asked the patient to draw what he'd seen. "His right hand drew a smiling face," Gazzaniga recalled. "'Why did you do that?' I asked. He said, 'What do you want, a sad face? Who wants a sad face around?'" The left hemisphere processes language, so the person encodes the word "face," but not the word "smile," which was flashed to the right side. However, that information is still encoded nonconsciously and he is able to draw a smiling face and come up with a post-hoc justification for it, without explicitly knowing that he was asked to draw a face with a smile.

The left-brain interpreter, Gazzaniga says, is what everyone uses to seek explanations for events, triage the barrage of incoming information, and construct narratives that help to make sense of the world.[5]

The Interpreter Module is an active, all-rationalizing-all-the-time participant in confabulation.[6] When asked to engage, it does; in fact, it's *always* ready unless you make it clear that it doesn't have to take the lead in a given circumstance. Creative thinking is one time it can take a break.

Ironically, it takes more conscious effort to reduce the predominance of the prefrontal cortex (PFC) and its executive function—that brain superhighway that helps you get from Point A to Point B as efficiently as possible. While we rely on this capability to make decisions and help us move forward, not every problem requires the speedy superhighway—in fact, creativity requires different tools and a more meandering approach.

"Transient hypofrontality" is the term for the temporary suppression of the PFC, which allows a more oblique approach to your creative work. We want to quiet down the PFC and wander through the lush fields of metaphor and explore unrelated side roads specifically because of their potential to help us stay off the well-paved superhighway. Some proactive messing around in the cul-de-sacs of the absurd will help us see what useful material we might discover. The tried-and-true PFC comes back into play when it's time to push ideas forward in hypothesis testing, but needs to be held at bay during Opportunity ID.

What you need to know to move forward at this stage will come through nonlinear play and then gradual synthesis, not premature extraction of "The Answer."

Ways to encourage Transient Hypofrontality include the following:

- **Engage The Visual, Engage The Emotional.** We're not talking regression back to primitive cave painting here, but our DNA has been prepped to understand and comprehend far more than straightforward verbal communications. By using images, graphics, and other visual stimuli, you can bypass the linear part of the brain to get at emotions and beliefs.

- **Use the Principle of Projection.** Make it safer for Ideation participants or focus group respondents to weigh in and slip by the Interpreter Module by eliciting information indirectly. There's a reason behind Rorschach tests. Asking, "What might a friend of yours who's concerned about this say?" and other approaches reduce concerns about judgment, or appearing less virtuous or intelligent. Going about it a different way, you can have fun with creative expressions, such as collages, poems, songs, one-act plays, or any other heartfelt creations that allow participants to express

things that matter deeply to them without arousing their self-con-
sciousness as a more direct approach can.

- **Thoughtful Laddering in a Group.** Ask "why?" or "What's good
  about that?" at least three times to drive more deeply to an underlying insight and to begin getting to root motivations. Many respondents will not have gone so deeply into their motivations, so it's
  important to select people who are more comfortable with going
  there, and to establish an environment that feels safe.

Create an Environment of Transparent Observation

Our default settings include: (1) interpreting when we believe we're just
observing and (2) wanting *The Answer* as soon as possible. The irony is
that both of these impede getting to the powerful insights you need—
those that get as close as possible to the Holy Grail of *obvious only in
hindsight* as previously discussed in Availability Bias. This is one of the
most important places to slow down in order to increase overall speed
in Time to Market Traction. Get the insights right up front and defend
them like a dog with a bone throughout, and you dramatically increase
the odds of market traction.

Transparent observation is the act of simply observing and listening to focus group participants without immediately interpreting their
words. Cultivating transparent observation is a great way to reduce con-
fabulation/overinterpretation, which may lead you further away from
the true insight.

Transparency is enhanced when we do the following:

- **Reward and Honor Transparency.** You need to establish a level
  of trust. Slow things down when you can tell the respondent is
  opening up to you in a truly human way. Do not blow past such

moments. Recognize the risk that they're taking, and thank them for it. Make it clear that their openness is appreciated, and will help create innovations that really get to their deepest needs. Give them psychological space to get more deeply into their emotions.

- **Just Observe.** Recognize that you'll slip into interpretation mode if you're not conscious of your tendency to do so. Try just observing for a while. Ask yourself if what you are about to say is merely an observation to open things up, or might it already have the tinge of an interpretation that might begin to close things down. Don't try to guess what's going on inside the respondents, at least too early on. What are you seeing and hearing on the outside? It's the Zen of Observation. When observing, just observe.

- **Get in Context.** When we rely exclusively on participants' memories to help us get to fruitful insight territory, we're increasing the likelihood of confabulation, and placing some bets that may not pay off. Shy of going straight to those Moments of Truth where product and performance intersect, there is much we can do in terms of diaries, videos, prep assignments, etc., to capture that helpful spontaneity. But there's nothing like being right there in the right context—the right place at the right moment. Other eyes will see other things. Other people with different backgrounds will have different stimuli available for them to process. When such ethnographic engagements happen, there will still be some confabulation, but we're arming you with ways to check it. Training of the observing team matters, and you'll have a more helpful experience if the subjects are screened and trained for ethnography as well. Subjects who are more emotionally aware and available, and have at least some basic creativity screening and training, will be more productive in getting you to insights that are unique and relevant, and that get closer to the gold standard of *obvious only in hindsight*.

- **Listen for More than Words, and with More than Your Ears.** Check to confirm that what you think is happening is indeed happening. Keep some humility about your interpretations—think of them more as speculations. Remember that the Interpreter Module is eager to make sense of what you're experiencing as soon as it can.

Think of how you respond to friends or loved ones who really need you to hear them. You're not merely trying to get information from their words, you're considering body language, tone of voice, eye contact, and the overall context. Bring some of that same care to the task of interacting with respondents. It's okay to speculate a little here. But regularly check to see if what you're taking away from it is what the respondent(s) intended to communicate. Imagine that the consumer is someone you're close to and care about.

Work with the Creatively Bold

Some consumers are naturally bold. Some can grow into boldness. By "creatively bold" we mean people who are comfortable with not appearing smarter or more virtuous than they are. They have enough sense of self to cop to some reality. You may notice in qualitative research that some respondents are confabulating or subconsciously hedging in the service of self-protection—even though they're unlikely to see each other or the moderator ever again. You can do things to lessen the likelihood of that noise in later testing. Don't worry too much about representative samples and solving it all up front. We're driving to *possibilities* here in Opportunity Identification, which matter more than the projectable sample of consumers we will need later. Find participants who naturally display the ability of give and take. These are people who are fine agreeing with others when that organically occurs, but don't need for that to happen to participate actively. The very nature of upfront work is to find *more* to consider, not *The Answer.*

Confabulation in Ideation

In Ideation—when divergence is the order of the day—confabulation is less of a snag because you're just looking for new ideas. You want quantity and stimulus. Recognize your tendency to rationalize what you're hearing and avoid doing so—just take it all in as stimulus without having to wrap an explanation to it. When judgment is suspended and you're not asking for justification or recall, confabulation is less of an issue. You still need to be grounded in your target audience and focused on potential ideas that meet a customer need, but if you have the right mix of creatively bold consumers, you can quickly push beyond the shallow layers to break newer ground that the Interpreter Module won't feel the need to rationalize.

Insight Development is one important reason why you should continue to work with the creatively bold consumer in Ideation (as opposed to straight-up Target Consumers later in the process when testing). We often begin a particular Target Area for Ideation by generating a round of Insights that deal with the Target Area topic. As with all our Insight work, we're chasing the holy grail of *obvious only in hindsight.* We need new, powerful articulations of what's motivating a particular consumer desire that will engender the "spontaneous head nod," followed by others' acknowledgment that they'd never thought of it that way. These trenchant Insights have that ring of truth precisely because they get past the feeling of being confabulated. There's a healthy feeling of "keeping it real" in a bold way that brings energy into the room and gets some great momentum going for Benefit expressions and Product possibilities that will use the Insights' energy to start pulling together exciting value propositions.

Confabulation in Concept Development

Confabulation can rear its well-intentioned head even more noticeably in the convergence process. Even when your stated goal is to go after innovation and to create change, confabulation can limit you to choosing only ideas that feel familiar or are most likely to be accepted by your group. You can start pulling together really important reasons why you can't go that far, perhaps focusing more on launch than learning. As discussed earlier, such negativity sounds very adult and responsible. Avoid it. Learning, not launch, is our design standard for the next steps of Testing.

How do you overcome this? Try to out-rationalize your rationalizations. Once you have converged, step back and talk about the key learning you had from Ideation as well as your criteria for convergence. By capturing the insights, aha moments, and implications, you can keep the newness top of mind. Another option is to plot out all your lead ideas and concepts on an axis that moves you from close-in ideas to stretched-beyond-comfort-level ideas. If you have too many close-ins, look to expand your selections to throw in a few wilder ideas. If you commit to accepting and moving some ideas from the less comfortable range forward, you might be surprised how well they are received. Be troubled at least a little by the idea of never getting to the learning that can place you apart from your category's conventional wisdom. Now is the time to put concepts forward that will help you get there.

Confabulation in Concept Testing

And now we've come to the typical focus group portion of confabulation. Think of six to eight strangers that have come together to talk about a topic for 60 to 120 minutes. These folks not only don't know each other, but are not likely ever to cross paths again. Absolute candor wouldn't seem to be a problem here, right? The screening should have already weeded out those who weren't likely to make a solid contribution to the group.

Earlier, we learned that we make rational-sounding reconstructions of events, feelings, fleeting sense impressions, etc., to make sense of our experiences for our own sanity. We can't avoid doing this. We don't intend to deceive, and we are not aware that we're distorting the truth. Just as docudramas start with the catch-all "based on actual events," many of our reports of events should be introduced with the same caveat.

So now respondents are being asked to consider something in much greater depth than ever before. They are even being paid a decent amount to opine. Not only do they *not* want to look dumb, they want to be helpful. And honest. But they may or may not know where they honestly land on some of the questions being thrown at them—it's not like we prepped them beforehand. Think about it like this: they are hearing about new ideas for the very first time so they don't know how they feel about them yet. And these are probably the same type of people who didn't like the idea of the iPad the very first time they heard about it, and now have three.

So how do you get past confabulation in Concept Testing?

Use Individual Input and Group Discussion for Their Respective Strengths. One of the first keys to getting around confabulation is to provide direction and allow for individual input. Hand out the concepts or briefs to each respondent and have them do individual processing.

Have them commit individually to an overall assessment as well as to dissect both what's working for them (even if they didn't like the overall idea much) and what's not working as well for them (even if they really liked the overall idea, get their help on making it even better). Have them mark up the sheet for any/all of the following:

- Overall assessment. We use a four-point system to avoid a fence-sitting midpoint and to gauge basic levels of interest. No premature quant-jocking happening here—the numbers are merely to facilitate a better qualitative conversation:

    4—Like it a lot
    3—Like it somewhat
    2—Dislike it somewhat
    1—Dislike it a lot

- What works (and why) and what doesn't work for them (and why).

- Any fixes for those things that don't work for them, or just overall opportunities to make the idea better, bumping "like" up to "love," an overall 2 to at least a 3, or a 3 to a 4, etc.

- Overall distilled idea (three to five words). Do they get the gist of it?

- New and different—again a four-point system:

    4—Very new and different
    3—Somewhat new and different
    2—Not very new and different
    1—Not new and different at all

It's important to give respondents the time to reflect on this and to mark down their initial responses. Reinforce that their honest response is the very most helpful thing here—not what they think we might want to hear, or what others might think, or what's going to go best with the group flow. Remind them a couple of times that while regular disagreement in a group discussion isn't natural for most of us, it's okay here if it's truly how individual respondents feel. The individual input approach is a great strategy for getting around premature group consensus (see the upcoming chapter on Conformity Bias), or the tendency to agree with whatever the first person said or the early input from a strong personality.

The learning in all of this will be unlocked by the power of *why*. It won't be nearly enough to hear what each person likes or dislikes—we can only surmise the motivations if we don't apply the shovel power of *why* to get what's going on under the surface. All the concept-detail *whats* are there to facilitate an enlightening *why* conversation. Think Rorschach test, not finished product. Concepts (and all prototypes) are only as good as the conversations that they get going, and *why* conversations are the important ones to have at this stage. Again, given our propensity to confabulate, it's helpful to remain humble about the conclusions we inevitably will start to draw.

How do you use a group for what a group can do better—and not for what it doesn't? Without securing individual thoughts and impressions first, groupthink is more likely to occur, led by the stronger voices. One thing the group *can* help with is to expose respondents to additional perspectives that may be helpful to their thought process. We're dealing with new ideas and many people need more time to consider them than the time available for each person in a focus group. Each respondent is likely to see a facet or two differently from anyone else in the group. As such, hearing each other out will make more considerations, both positive and negative, available to each respondent. When more perspectives are shared to help all consider that the reality might be a little more complex than their individual opinion, but not foremost to change minds, we get a richer conversation. It isn't a contest to find out who's right, but a conversation to help the client team understand more fully what the opportunities and challenges actually are. Agreement, whenever it occurs, is fine but not necessary. Some amount of disconfirmation of individual opinions is very helpful, particularly when the *why* shovel goes to work. Again, use the group to get more consideration, not necessarily *the answer.*

Extract, but Also Synthesize. Don't forget to synthesize. Verbatims from qualitative research to illustrate a key point of learning are awesome. Verbatims in isolation as the learning itself, are less so. Listen for themes as well as specifics. Both are helpful to pull together the learning. Since much of our communication is non-verbal, be sure to watch body language (but don't be too quick to interpret it) and listen for inflection and tonality.

For broad thematic learning, ask yourself what was true across the following:

- Multiple concepts—the big, general learning.

- Multiple respondents (and *why* . . . no we're not skipping that anytime soon!).

- Multiple groups—always important to do more than one to isolate the "One Weird Group" issue.

This is just input, and doesn't relieve your team from taking responsibility for decisions that will be necessary afterward. You have access to other research and other experiences that can help you use testing appropriately. Think Bayesian inference—each new input updates the estimate of probability. You've collected a little more evidence and are still building the plan. This output, itself, is not the plan. There's work to do yet.

Remember Ogilvy's Lamppost. The godfather of modern advertising, David Ogilvy, said something wise about the correct use of research. Don't use it, he said, as a drunk uses a lamppost—for support rather than illumination. Confabulation also affects us as we try to make sense of all that we hear during testing. Remember, though, we are programmed as humans to pull together the plausible story prematurely. Actively seek out disconfirmation. (Remember the number-sequence game in the Confirmation Bias chapter?) You'll learn more. Support comes later as you build the case for your next steps. Right now, get all the illumination you can, and hope for beneficial surprises that break through the bounds of your assumptions. Doubt anything that smells even a little pat. Keep things open and stay humble for a little bit.

7

Conformity Bias—
Play Along to Get Along

"The opposite for courage is not cowardice, it is conformity.
Even a dead fish can go with the flow."

—Jim Hightower

CAMERA ZOOMS IN ON A PREHISTORIC CLAN COUNCIL. AS CLOSE AS we can translate, it goes something like this:

Atouk (the clan's general-purpose go-between member): "Og, we think it would be super if you could support us on this woolly mammoth expedition we're trying to assemble here, man. We've heard your protestations on the risk-reward balance, and that a sustained effort mounted against squirrels would actually net us a steadier source of protein *and* let more of us return unharmed. But Cha-Ka has weighed in, and, well, you know how things go once Cha-Ka speaks. How about it, huh? We'd really like your support on this. I mean, I'd hate for you and your family to miss out on all that mammoth meat, and . . . pssst . . . (very quietly) . . . you can keep the squirrel thing going on after hours, but be discreet, dude!"

Og: "Okay."

Getting along with the group has been such an indispensable skill for most of our history that our brain still pushes back if we buck the system too much. We are still hardwired for group agreement. We see it so clearly when our kids defend their latest desire by saying "everyone else is doing it." And what is the classic retort? "If everyone else was going to jump off the bridge, would you do *that*?" You will notice that we never get a response, because they probably would! Conformity is the root of that pernicious peer pressure that our teenagers insist doesn't exist (because it operates outside of *their* awareness). It's the unofficial dress code that develops in every group and every workplace. It's the target of Henry David Thoreau's scathing critique in *Walden* of the fashion industry, "The head monkey at Paris puts on a traveler's cap, and all the monkeys in America do the same." And we would like to believe that we are somehow beyond these social pressures. We are not.

As further evidence of the evolutionary genetics of conformity, disagreeing with the group is associated with higher levels of cortisol—the stress hormone that triggers the fight-or-flight response.[1] We feel it when we buck the system, as a signal that we'd better be ready for a fight. It was evolutionarily adaptive to be alerted by our bodies that any break with authority was dangerous. But we have seen what happens when our bodies do our thinking for us (remember System 1). The less conscious mode of functioning can be very quick and perceptive, but not very thoughtful. There are times when we would clearly benefit from the well-reasoned resources of System 2. And why not have the best of both worlds: let System 1 send the signal that it could be dangerous to break away from the pack, and use System 2 to decide whether that course of action will lead to being abandoned by the market, or being a market leader, taking the entire industry into a whole new dimension of product development.

In the context of innovation work, we often do the group a bigger favor by bracketing conformity for a while and consciously seeking diverging viewpoints, fresh perspectives, and deliberate dissent. It helps, of course, if everyone in the group agrees to this approach! And see how our need for conformity is so ubiquitous that we even seek approval from the group to temporarily suspend our conformity!

Conformity is the hallmark of the status quo. Innovation is, by definition, a break with conformity to establish a "new" status quo that better serves the needs of the group in ways that are *obvious only in hindsight*. The unconscious tug of conformity will stall innovation throughout the process, from Opportunity ID and Ideation to Concept Development, and even on through launch.

Worrying too much about consensus early in the new-product-development process will hamper our efforts to explore new dimensions of the Uniqueness and Relevance we need to keep our company and brands thriving. Even further down the development funnel, as we get closer to launch, the absence of diverging perspectives can be deadly, as pressures to toe the line will often trump an important concern. A few case studies here illustrate the point:

This pressure to conform, it can been argued, helped cause Ford employees to sell the Pinto despite awareness of its gas tank dangers, and helped A. H. Robins employees continue to sell the Dalkon Shield contraceptive IUD despite knowing its ghastly medical consequences.

The impairment of individual decision making known as "groupthink"—where people deciding in groups often make more extreme decisions than any individual member initially supports—can exacerbate the Conformity Bias. It can be reasonably argued that loyalty and groupthink helped Morton Thiokol employees to remain silent about known O-ring dangers that caused the Challenger Space Shuttle disaster.[2]

We need to be very conscious about how we balance the ultimate need for agreement with a healthy clash of perspectives. Neither conformity nor divergence are necessarily good or bad themselves. There is a time and place for each, but you should consider the value of more perspectives throughout the process of New Product Development. The need to build consensus and conformity can always come later. Solve for Uniqueness first, and then retool for Relevance.

Let's be clear. Unity in purpose is essential. Agreeing to the basic direction of your innovation work is indispensable. But real damage is done by a hastily cobbled-together consensus. It preempts the innovation process. By seeking agreement prematurely at the expense of diversity, we end up blending into the background. Consensus on that which not only doesn't need consensus, but is actually harmed by premature consensus . . . no. No. Please.

We figured out as a species millennia ago that incest wasn't a particularly successful genetic strategy. Expanding the "idea genetic pool" and having a vigorous consideration of multiple viewpoints is equally healthy for our innovation efforts. The famous philosopher of social, political, and economic theory, John Stuart Mill, expounds on the value of multiple perspectives. In the following quote from *On Liberty*, he notes that the rush to consensus hurts the group as much as it does the individual who is challenging the prevailing ways:

> . . . the peculiar evil of silencing the expression of an opinion is, that it is robbing the human race; posterity as well as the existing generation; those who dissent from the opinion, still more than

those who hold it. If the opinion is right, they are deprived of the opportunity of exchanging error for truth: if wrong, they lose, what is almost as great a benefit, the clearer perception and livelier impression of truth, produced by its collision with error.

Even this eminent philosopher recognizes the evolutionary implications of conformity, across generations. He also notes that any productive challenge of a group's conformity is a win-win. We either get to correct an error or fortify our commitment to the truth.

It is necessary to consider separately these two hypotheses, each of which has a distinct branch of the argument corresponding to it. We can never be sure that the opinion we are endeavouring to stifle is a false opinion; and if we were sure, stifling it would be an evil still.[3]

Supreme Court Justice Louis Brandeis elaborated on this theme in his strident defense of the freedom of speech for the benefit of the listeners as much as the speakers:

No danger flowing from speech can be deemed clear and present, unless the incidence of the evil apprehended is so imminent that it may befall before there is opportunity for full discussion. If there be time to expose through discussion the falsehood and fallacies, to avert the evil by the processes of education, *the remedy to be applied is more speech*, not enforced silence.[4]

Brandeis is clearly saying that the only danger associated with the airing of any opinion is that it may be accepted without opportunities for further discussion of the issues at hand. The "bird in the hand" becomes all too quickly attractive. And this is as true in innovation as it is in politics and philosophy.

We need more ideas up front in any effort, not fewer. We need to leverage the power of the group to provide more perspectives and generate more possibilities by feeding off each other than any member of the group could generate alone. Even when an idea doesn't work for us, that deficiency may be an opportunity to consider something that had never crossed our mind before. Even if we disagree with all or part of the idea, its expression may have put something on the table that could be very important, and maybe—just maybe—will crack open a very productive space. Spend some time here. More variation up front makes us much smarter in the eventual selection.

A dog's "electric fence" collar is the metaphor here. It takes only a couple of shocks for us to understand where the group wants us to (wait for it . . .) "stay" and if lucky, not roll over or play dead. We internalize these invisible boundaries as if they were the highest barriers and too often satisfy ourselves with all we can do within the safe zone. This sometimes happens even if we're encouraged to go past the limits. The pull to stay within the territory in which the group is comfortable is powerful.

Conformity Bias in Opportunity ID

The Cognitive Biases and other obstacles we've discussed throughout this book are mostly abstract and not limited to a particular person or group. However, your company might have a person or group whose specific responsibility may be what we've sarcastically referred to as "Innovation Prevention." As discussed earlier, risk is often limited to concerns about commission, not omission, and some of your colleagues build job security by making sure that your company never plays around with anything containing a whiff of risk. That, of course, would include anything that's sufficiently new, weird, or possibly destabilizing to the "unwritten order of things." Your job as an innovationista is to promote wise risk; they may feel their job is to keep you from doing anything.

So, how do we get around these "corporate antibodies" that your culture may see as vital to maintaining a healthy "corporate immune system"?

Assistors/Resistors. Kurt Lewin taught that "An issue is held in balance by the interaction of two opposing sets of forces—those seeking to promote change (driving forces) and those attempting to maintain the status quo (restraining forces)."[5] His "Force Field" model shows that progress can happen only through strengthening the driving forces and/or weakening the restraining forces.

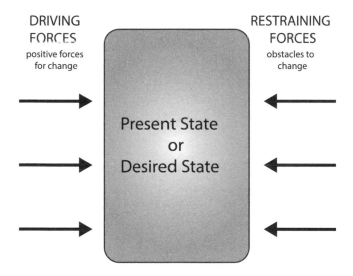

DRIVING FORCES
positive forces for change

RESTRAINING FORCES
obstacles to change

Present State
or
Desired State

Accept the reality of these restraining forces in your company so you can more effectively promote the change you need to as a self-respecting innovation professional.

To avoid polarizing your opponent, enter the dialogue with some empathy. Go in with the idea that no one in the "Innovation Prevention

Department" gets up in the morning and immediately begins conspiring to make your job more difficult. You need to understand where they're coming from, maybe even better than they do. They truly believe they're doing the right thing to defend and support the organization or their superiors. Charlie Munger of Berkshire Hathaway said, "I never allow myself to have an opinion on anything that I don't know the other side's argument better than they do. You must force yourself to consider arguments on the other side." Munger also offers that "We all are learning, modifying, or destroying ideas all the time. Rapid destruction of your ideas when the time is right is one of the most valuable qualities you can acquire."[6] Some self-scrutiny about your own need to see others as the opposition is a great place to start. Remember, you are likely to be most wrong when you consider yourself to be most right.

The more empowering approach is to wonder how you can find common ground. Or if you can't quite suppress your subversive streak, start plotting how you can co-opt the position of your opponent. If you can't have some fun with this, you need to reconsider some of your priorities.

What's behind their position? Given the notion that no one is capable of 100 percent error, what important point is the different perspective addressing that you perhaps haven't considered sufficiently? As Rule #1 in improv says, "Whatever arises, use it!" By doing so, you have the opportunity to strengthen the current thinking.

Back to Lewin's Force Field model. Consider the classic journalists' questions of "Who, What, When, Where, Why, and How" as they pertain to both your Assistors and Resistors to your innovation efforts.

The roles of Assistor and Resistor are not limited to people. Corporate policies can be even more obstructive than the people who wrote them. Innovationistas and marketers have been known to assume that policies and regulations are more ironclad than they actually are. Push the limits (tactfully) and see what develops. Taking the battle another way, you can also exploit the idiosyncrasies of your corporate culture by finding a precedent for flexibility or dissension in a particular area.

You want to acknowledge the Conformity Bias in others and show that you're a good corporate citizen while still embodying the spirit of the "raging, inexorable thunderlizard evangelist" persona that Guy Kawasaki enlisted for the launch of the original Apple Macintosh. Stay true to the cause without inadvertently triggering a powerful immune response within the corporate body.

To prepare your approach to any innovative effort, list at least twelve Assistors and twelve Resistors. Pick the top five within each group to explore in greater depth. Amp up your curiosity about each of these and be open to the idea that you may not understand all you need to know about them. Go beyond the obvious by using the journalistic inquiry to ask forty or more questions such as the following:

- What potential Assistors can we learn about from companies in other industries with even more onerous regulations that *still* find a way to innovate consistently? If you're in the food industry, for example, and deal with the US Food & Drug Administration, what could you learn from the additional scrutiny that the FDA gives the pharmaceutical industry?

- Which Assistor seems to be increasing in organizational power and how can we strengthen it further? What's most like that which you're already working on, and who or what in the company has helped out under similar circumstances?

- Who can help us with this Resistor? What's lessening the impact of this Resistor like?

- Who has this Resistor's ear (when a person or role is clearly seen as resistance)?

- How did our last big breakthrough happen despite facing the same internal constraints?

- When does everyone seem to hide behind a particular Resistor policy, and when are they more open to finding a way around it?

And as you start pulling together potential Target Areas to explore in Ideation, use this model to be really smart about the time you'll spend. How might you avoid blind alleys that some of the "Yes, But-ters" on your team might call out prematurely, but still set yourself up to explore Unique areas? But don't be tempted to use this model to shrink your areas of exploration. Use it to optimize where you'll go for Ideation and further development. Anticipate the road ahead, and the roadblocks you may encounter, remembering that you're helping to create your company's future. Do not abdicate that responsibility.

The Force Field model is also a great tool when you get past Concept Testing and want to start drawing up Action Plans. Use it to plot your strategy. While you have your team together during the debrief from testing, for example, get real about next steps. Now is the time to be frank and (dare we say) helpfully conspiratorial about making something great happen. Acknowledge Resistor elephants in the room (or the organization) and see how you can start co-opting the forces to keep the momentum. Innovation is "the good war." Get a little Eisenhower on it.

Conformity in Ideation

There are several ways to alleviate fears in Ideation. The first—and really most simple—is setting the right environment. A safe environment consists of both the physical setting and the mindset of the group. As we discussed in Negativity Bias, *Forness* thinking can help people offer ideas in a low-risk way by knowing that any objections to their ideas will be introduced with the softer, forward-looking preface, "I wish for . . . " or "Wouldn't it be great if . . . " This lets people express alternative thoughts and insights without worrying about too much feather-ruffling.

The physical setting is also important. In every Ideation session, we arrange the room in a semicircle of comfy chairs. Remember "circle time" when you were a kid? Or King Arthur's "round table"? It's all about conveying inclusiveness and openness. It just might be difficult to "think outside the box" when sitting at a square table. Arranging an arc of chairs in the room may actually produce an upward arc of ideas in the session. According to Osborn's theory about the quantity and quality of ideas, the rate of good ideas will increase in a curvilinear arc as Ideation continues.[7] Essentially, Osborn believed that "the ratio of good ideas to total ideas would increase as more ideas are generated, resulting in increasing returns for additional ideas."[8]

One of the most effective ways to increase the quantity and diversity of ideas is to reduce the fear of looking foolish among the group. Circular sitting also encourages the "rolling out" of ideas, versus the back-and-forth that can occur when opponents face each other directly. Sitting side-by-side increases the sense of solidarity without encouraging conformity. Nonlinear room, nonlinear thinking—you get the idea.

Another hedge against conformity in Ideation is to stoke the diversity of the "ideators." Adding input in the same direction will actually work against blazing new trails. You can chart more territory by bringing in people with divergent views and interests. You want consumers who can think and emote independently. In a classic study conducted at the University of Michigan, heterogeneity among group members stimulated more complex thinking, better problem solving, and greater creativity. We are particularly fond of introducing consumers who are naive about the subject area. We often suggest a client consider including children in an Ideation session or adding a stay-at-home dad to a new moms' Ideation group. You can bring homogeneous, algorithm-based consumers back in during qualitative evaluation, but it is important to push for outside perspectives that can add richness and Uniqueness during Ideation.

And don't stop with the heterogeneity of the consumers. It is equally important to build diversity in the team that is tasked with the innovation initiatives. We always recommend that our clients assemble a multifunctional team for Ideation—everyone from marketing managers, market researchers, product development folks, creative agencies, even sales team members who often have the most direct contact with end buyers. Sometimes the naïveté of each function regarding the behind-the-scenes issues of the other functions can open teams up to explore more possibilities.

Beyond the value of diverse roles, it's critically important to include different styles of creativity. Including each of the classic styles of creativity will increase the likelihood of success. "Innovative dreamers" challenge the team. "Synthesizers" can extrapolate the unexpected from what is known. "Planners" help make things happen when the time is right. It's no surprise that assumptions are sometimes made related to roles on a team. You may want to consider including any additional styles that you've noticed along the creativity spectrum .

In assembling the right team members for Ideation, pause for a moment to recognize that their creative style may not be predicted by their role in the organization. Such assumptions and stereotypes obscure their potentials for creativity. For example, at the start of a recent project, an R&D lead jokingly introduced herself as "The Dream Killer." As the project progressed she unexpectedly met every snag with, "What if we . . . ?" The team was obliged and delighted to rechristen her "The Dream Maker." Her unique perspective and creative style were just as important as her traditional area of expertise. And this tweak in the redefinition of her role as part of a creative team is one of the things that make being an innovationista so rewarding.

Conformity in Concept Development

Have you ever seen a really exciting idea get gradually watered down to the point where it barely resembles the original concept that was once so exciting? A "sure hit" becomes a "no-go" and everyone wonders "what happened?" Upon closer examination, you might have noticed that the team was genuinely excited about the original idea, but the Conformity Bias led to a gradual regression toward "the commonplace," and they let "ho-hum" ideas slide without speaking up because they didn't want to make waves so late in the process. For this reason, you want people in the group who are not afraid to make waves, but will still take direction when a thoughtful facilitator tries to limit contributions that are truly disruptive. It takes a special consumer group to achieve this balance, and an experienced consultant to assemble such a group.

Embrace dissent. Groups often don't rise to the level of effectiveness that we'd expect from the sum of the individuals. The push for a hastily constructed consensus is often the culprit. This "strain for consensus" often overprivileges the influence of the majority and creates silence in the minority and in any members of the majority who might prefer to kick things around a bit more. Working so hard for premature consensus can create polarization as views become extreme. We sometimes double down on the supposed fitness/unfitness of an adopted course of action, depending on our status as majority supporters or minority dissenters.

Antergy (or antagonism, both commonly used antonyms for synergy) describes the too-common phenomenon of the end result being less than the sum of the parts. In antergy, 2 + 2 = 3 or less, vs. the hoped-for synergy of 2 + 2 = 5 or greater. Antergy seems unacceptable—why not just keep people acting separately if combining them lowers performance?

Where does that extra value go when we're talking about teams working in concept development? The lost value may be in the options not considered, the experience and perspective of others not exploited, and new territory never being imagined. Simply put, value is lost through a failure to set up and use the potential power of additional perspectives and experience.

We can do better. Research shows that dissent plays a very important role, helping to "liberate individuals from conformity pressures and, more important, can stimulate thought that considers more information and more options and culminates in better decision making and productivity."[9]

While dissent for its own sake can undermine the group and diminish morale, dissenting points of view can enrich the group when introduced and incorporated effectively. Whenever possible, try to increase the number of options on the table. Guard against Availability Bias by helping the group search far and wide for diversity. Keep the ideas on the table as long as possible so they can continue to multiply. Try to delay the natural drift from "possibilities to be explored" to "nominees to be endorsed" in a premature vote on action.

When it's time to winnow the options, we can learn a lot from the principles of structured debate. Experienced debaters learn how to argue effectively and passionately in favor of opposing positions. In this way, they develop a much more nuanced appreciation for the merits of the other side. In his classic work, *Six Thinking Hats*, Edward de Bono designates the Black Hat as the "judgment hat" for all of the members of the group to mentally put on together and play the Devil's Advocate by spotting dangers and poking holes in faulty arguments. It's important in de Bono's process for everyone to walk through all the important perspectives together, including the Black Hat, at the right time. That way no one person is the "bad guy" and everyone has an opportunity to voice their concerns.

In Concept Development, make sure you balance the courage of your convictions with a healthy dose of humility. "Strong opinions, loosely held" is the ideal here. This means avoiding the extremes of either rubberstamping something or blowing it all away. Care enough about your position to extract all the benefit you can, then make sure you're open to the perspectives of others. No one member of the group should dominate the rest. The products of a healthy group will always be greater than the sum of the individual contributions.

Conformity in Concept Testing

Redefine "groupthink." You see Conformity in action in focus groups all the time. Once the discussion begins, individual opinions can become muddled into a subtle form of "groupthink." We are, by nature, consensus-seeking creatures. As we discussed in confabulation, it's important to make sure participants commit to their opinions by writing them down and/or saying them aloud to the group before the discussion ensues. As Conformity is so quick to emerge, remind respondents, supportively and at least a couple of times, that their initial individual response is important to hear, and that getting that out on the table is more important than everyone making nice. Acknowledge that it is, indeed, unusual behavior to disagree, even with strangers when the personal stakes would seem to be so low. The job of the moderator is to ensure that the interpersonal environment supports such counterintuitive behavior, so that more honest initial reactions can be gathered.

The story of the *Abilene Paradox* illustrates a kind of groupthink that you might find painfully familiar:

> On a hot afternoon in Coleman, Texas, the family is comfortably playing dominoes on a porch, until the father-in-law suggests that they take a trip to Abilene (fifty-three miles north) for dinner. The wife says, "Sounds like a great idea." The husband, despite having reservations because the drive is long and hot, thinks that his preferences must be out-of-step with the group and says, "Sounds good to me. I just hope your mother wants to go." The mother-in-law then says, "Of course I want to go. I haven't been to Abilene in a long time."
>
> The drive is hot, dusty and long. When they arrive at the cafeteria, the food is as bad as the drive. They arrive back home four hours later, exhausted.
>
> One of them dishonestly says, "It was a great trip, wasn't it?" The mother-in-law says that, actually, she would rather have stayed home, but went along since the other three were so enthusiastic. The husband says, "I wasn't delighted to be doing what we were doing. I only went to satisfy the rest of you." The wife says, "I just went along to keep you happy. I would have had to be crazy to want to go out in the heat like that." The father-in-law then says that he only suggested it because he thought the others might be bored.

The group sits back, perplexed that they together decided to take a trip which none of them wanted. They each would have preferred to sit comfortably, but did not admit to it when they still had time to enjoy the afternoon.[10]

Sometimes it just seems easier to go with the crowd, even if no one is particularly thrilled with where the crowd is going. You've seen it. A particularly thorny problem presents itself. No one can agree on a solution because each solution can be somewhat controversial. Someone finally proposes a solution that is least controversial and relatively safe. The other members of the group gradually agree. Some are relieved that *something* is on the table. Everyone conforms and they compromise their way out of innovation. Ironically, no one is particularly happy with the outcome. *Forness* thinking is your tool of choice here. By encouraging members of the group to articulate what they "wish for," they can break with conformity without the social consequences of being oppositional. It's pretty useful, don't you think? (It's okay to disagree here in an "I wish" form if you need to.) Push to find alternatives to make it better.

A metaphor from genetics might be helpful here. Denise Caruso of *The Whole Earth Catalog* described "hybrid vigor" as "the good juju that happens at the edges of a field when pollen from wild plants mingles with the cultivated ones, thereby increasing the strength and yield of the crops."[11] We're acutely aware of the consequences of inbreeding, what with the well-known hip dysplasia in some pedigreed dogs and some of the misadventures of the House of Windsor. (Hey, one small jab from the Colonials, huh?) The best option is often neither of the binary left-right, but is found *through* them both on the other side where important parts of each are pulled together into a smarter, more satisfying third alternative. It takes a little more work, sure. But take some time to understand what third alternatives you could generate, and then select the one that best honors and incorporates as much as possible from conflicting perspectives.[12]

8

Confirmation Bias—
Just as I Thought!

"All of (subpopulation X) walk in single file—
at least the one I saw did."

—Colloquialism from 70s American West

WE LOVE RULES, ESPECIALLY THE ONES THAT HELP US UNDERSTAND
how things work. We often infer them subconsciously. It helps us predict
what's going to happen in similar situations later. We love to feel we have
the lay of the land.

Let's play a game.[1] I have a rule in my mind for a sequence of three
numbers, and I'll give you one sequence that fits this rule: 2, 4, 6. I want
you to propose other three-number sequences to test what you think the
rule might be. I'll let you know if it fits my rule or not, but I want you to
guess what you think the rule might be—this is the object of the game.

Where do you go first? What would be a good set of numbers to test
in order to add to your knowledge about this game? Stop for a moment

and actually think of three numbers that might be consistent with the rule I'm using in the sequence of 2, 4, 6. Commit!

If you're like the participants in a study conducted by Peter Wason, you're likely to default to a strategy that *confirms* your hypothesis. Most people will start with "8, 10, 12" or "20, 22, 24" because they believe they are responding to "a sequence of even numbers," or more specifically, "a sequence of *consecutive* or *increasing* even numbers." What if you guessed: "4, 186, 542"? That gives you more information because you could rule out whether the numbers need to be evenly spaced. The objective is not to guess what numbers come next, but to identify the rule behind the original sequence. Go wild. How about trying "3, 24, 97"? That guess will at least help you understand if "even numbers" are baked into the rule.

In fact, each of the above responses fits the rule—but you're learning more about the rule the moment you break it, not by repeatedly reaffirming it. Testing the rule with what you already think you know merely supports your assumptions and can lead to false confidence that can actually reduce the acuity of your perceptions. Break away quickly from the assumptions of even/odd or consecutive numbers right away. Then try . . . get ready for this . . . decreasing numbers, or something like "1, 5, 4," which at least mixes up increasing and decreasing.

The rule used in the Wason research is merely this—increasing numbers. "1, 100, 982" fits. So does the close-in first guess that most make. But those first attempts didn't add anything to our getting closer to figuring out the rule. We succumbed to Confirmation Bias.

Confirmation Bias is the tendency for people to favor information that supports their existing beliefs and ignore information that contradicts it. Put in innovation terms, just because you build it (and you think it's great), does not mean your customers will agree.

Think about who your customers are. You are probably not one of them, even if your demographics, psychographics, etc., seem to conform to your target definition. One mistake that Confirmation Bias often uncovers is that many marketers think that simply because they are consumers, they are also *their* own consumers. While we should all accept that we need to understand consumers in order to innovate, we can't model innovation on only the details that we think are great. Beyond that, because you are only one person, there is no reason your views are typical. Just because you like a particular feature, doesn't mean most people in the same consumer segment as you would like it too. The fact is, mainstream consumers (or even niche consumers) may fit an entirely different profile. Again, some humility helps. Don't be too quick to believe you have cornered the truth.

And it's just in our nature to try to find more evidence to support what we already believe to be true. Given finite resources of time and cognitive effort, we skip the opportunity to *disconfirm*, and bolster what we already believe (or even just "know") to be true.

Going back to the number game, a deliberate strategy to *disprove*, or, as Karl Popper puts it, *falsify* your hypothesis is a more efficient way to gain knowledge. Beat up your hypotheses, don't coddle them. This is huge for innovation—those companies that set out to test their hypotheses stringently, hoping to abandon them for better hypotheses, will win.

Path Dependence

Fewer than 20 percent of calls to most fire departments are about fires; the majority require responses to medical emergencies, traffic accidents, and other situations. But they're still called fire departments and have much of their training and infrastructure tied to firefighting. Fire departments came together to handle the obvious risks associated with cities constructed of flammable materials, mainly wood. In modern urban settings, we're dealing much more with nonflammable materials such as concrete and steel. The name "fire department" is a vestige of our highly combustible past. The entrepreneur Paul Kedrosky amplifies another author's observation in this regard: "The writer William Gibson once famously said, 'The future is already here—it's just not very evenly distributed.' I worry more that the past is here—it's just so evenly distributed that we can't get to the future."[2]

We become dependent on the path already paved. You may have heard the story linking the width of space shuttle booster rockets back to the width of horses' rear ends. We can step backward in time to see how the previous decision constrained options thereafter. The booster rockets were held to the constraint of railroad tunnel height and width, since that would be their means of transport to Cape Canaveral. Railroad tunnel dimensions were, naturally, based on the width of railroad tracks, whose width was based on the dimensions of railroad cars, which used horse-drawn wagons as a model, given their "go-to" status of all that was right and good within the realm of transport conveyances at that time. Horse-drawn wagons were, of course, tied to the width of two horses' rear ends, which was also tied to chariot width and thus road widths throughout the Roman Empire. While that sounds humorously weird, it shouldn't surprise us that much. We are resourceful critters who regularly try to apply old solutions to emerging needs. It's understandable that railroad widths would land somewhere in a tight range around the width of vehicles pulled by horses. Rail engines were even called "iron horses" in the early days, and we called cars "horseless carriages" early in automobile history. We go with what we already know.

If we don't make a conscious effort to identify and prevent the Confirmation Bias, what we already know will limit what, and even if, we will learn from "new" information and experience. In fact, we won't even recognize the information as "new." Your best bets in the early stages of innovation are a series of tools that keep you asking, "How do I know that?" and "Why do I think that?"

Think of the royal courtiers in "The Emperor's New Clothes." They *all* knew what was going on. They quickly figured out how to discount anything that would suggest that the Emperor's finery wasn't made of only the most exquisite materials, even when the truth was (ahem . . .) on display right in front of them *all the time!* No one wanted to acknowledge the terrible truth. There's a metaphor with some punch.

Confirmation Bias in Opportunity ID

Diversity of perspective matters in Opportunity Identification. As we talked about in Conformity Bias, getting multiple functions in your company involved early in an innovation project helps reduce the probability of merely confirming what you already think you know to be true. Not only do multiple perspectives cover more ground, they also identify opportunities and concerns more efficiently and effectively. We have found that innovation teams with high diversity of thought outperform those with low diversity by more than double in the early stages of the innovation process. Opportunity ID is the place to begin considering much more—it's where deadline pressures are typically not as great (fingers crossed). Diversity of perspective is a shortcut to a much broader consideration space.

Typical Process:
Jump to solution based on one view of the challenge

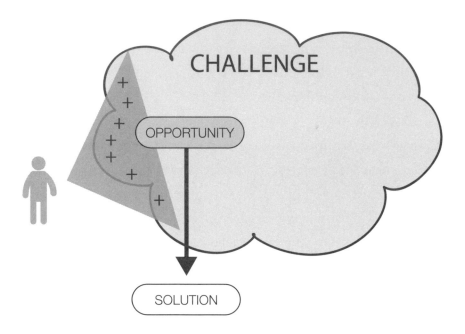

Obviously, to come up with better (new) solutions to the problems you encounter during development, you must go beyond incremental ideas. We need to consider the possibility that our view of the world, the market, or our product category might need shaking up. Since our human tendency is to retain and support existing models, you need to consciously be doing things to help you and your team break out of this natural limitation on new thinking.

So, now you have an idea. Possibly a great idea. You've heard from some customers that this idea is worth pursuing. It's time to develop and hone it now. Unfortunately, it's all too easy to succumb to the Cognitive Biases that can lead to homogenizing that once great idea. We have to be very careful to continue to innovate creative solutions to the problems we encounter during development, so we don't end up turning what was a unique and relevant idea into just another flavor of what already exists.

Opportunity Expansion:

Results in seeing the challenge through many different lenses.
Results in more opportunity for better solutions.

To illustrate how this can easily happen, we have the creative tension model introduced by Peter Senge. This is a mental model that helps you think about creativity and change. Creative tension occurs when the gap between a clearly articulated vision and a realistic picture of the current reality becomes clear. This creates an emotional and energetic tension that we as humans seek to resolve. Think about a rubber band stretched between your two hands. The tendency of the stretched rubber band is to contract to resolve the tension. Imagine that the vision is represented by your right hand and the current reality is your left hand. The goal of creative problem solving is to ensure that the tension is resolved by moving your left hand (current reality) toward your right hand (the vision), rather than allowing the vision to get diluted to be closer to current reality.[3]

This is the trap we see all too often in this phase. If the envisioned new product won't run on the current production line, we change the product slightly so that it will. If the margin isn't quite where we need it to be, we change the product slightly so that it is. If the really unique feature is too expensive, we change it slightly to reduce the cost. Unfortunately, this iterative watering down of the initial idea also reduces its Uniqueness and Relevance. As we make several changes over the course of development, we can eventually wind up with a product that has lost its "wow."

To help overcome Confirmation Bias, regularly introduce new data, new experiences, new vendors, and new solutions. Our company frequently brings into innovation sessions people we call Adjacent Experts. These are people who have expertise in a related but different area than our clients'. For example, bring other perspectives into your insight discovery and idea generation processes. We once invited a boat designer, a rainwater management expert, a sculptor, and a water-park designer (among others) to help generate new packaging and product ideas for a beverage company. The project team was amazed at the range and diversity of new ideas they got when they were exposed to the new perspectives on their challenge. They got to ideas they never would have thought of on their own—simply due to their embedded assumptions about the topic. We see in this a creative counter for both Confirmation and Availability Biases.

Don't rely on conventional data to understand your customers' needs. You need to actually talk to them. Go to their homes or offices to witness the problems they need solved. All too often we have clients call for a problem-solving session and say, "We don't need to do any customer work as part of this; we already have 'lots of data.'" This always makes us wary, because it usually means they have reams of statistics about customers. Unfortunately, it rarely means they have any real insight into customer needs. If you're expecting your team to understand the customer by reading a PowerPoint deck or attending a presentation, challenge yourself to find a more engaging and interactive process. It will be far more effective to immerse your team in the real customer experience to help them develop their own understanding of their customer.

Confirmation Bias in Ideation

In Ideation, we're fleshing out big opportunity areas from Opportunity ID. Great, innovatively defined opportunity areas (going beyond category assumptions) coming out of that critical work already give us a great start on innovation, and it's on us now to keep the freshness of thinking going. Here are a couple of exercises to keep us from lapsing back into what everybody already believes they know.

Takeover is a way to force associations that will deliberately take you away from the tractor-beam pull of Confirmation Bias. Imagine that a deliberately diverse crew of interesting people came to partner with you on a new opportunity area. Here are some details:

This exercise is like a doing a role-play with a fictitious mentor. Forget about how you would launch your new service or product. Forget about how your company would do it. Think about how someone else would do it. How would Tiffany launch your cereal bar? How would JetBlue launch your new checking account product? How would Eastern Mountain Sports launch your eyeglass collection? How would Starbucks launch your car?

1. Get into the mindset and tonality of the mentor brand. Write down all of the things that make that brand what it is (what it's like, how it's perceived, who gravitates toward it).

2. Look for the types of things the mentor brand has done that have been successful. What type of media do they use? How to they use it? What does their grassroots campaign look like? How are they using social media?

3. Then adapt what they are doing to your brand and try something different. To make the most of this exercise, don't just do the closest-in co-branding, or "The Signature Collection from Celebrity X," but use what's behind their success to get you thinking more deeply about your opportunities. It's less about doing precisely what they do, and much more about seeking what they seek. Use the principles and ingenuity behind their success, not their bling. And, as with all creative excursions, you don't need to prove the elegance or linearity of your thought process—this is just to get you out of the obvious and expected.

For this example, imagine you're in the business of supplying something superfunctional such as the rings that hold shower curtains to the curtain rod, and that you've identified the opportunity to bring additional sensory benefit to the shower environment. Curtain rings are exposed to temperature and humidity differences, to movement as the shower curtain is drawn back, etc. There are actually a few things going on in the entire shower experience that maybe you haven't considered as potential sources of innovation. Let's stretch your thinking further with a list of interesting, unrelated people or companies to partner with—deliberately chosen to stretch your thinking and get you past the easiest, most immediate associations that you might have with more well-known people:

- Rosalind Franklin, chemist and X-ray crystallographer who made critical contributions to the understanding of the fine molecular structures of DNA, RNA, viruses, coal, and graphite.

- The folks from the Positive Deviance Initiative, an NGO applying the insight that outliers in any community achieve outsized positive results while facing the same constraints as the rest of the population.

- Hedy Lamarr, actor and co-inventor of spread spectrum and frequency-hopping communications technology for the military.

- Norman Borlaug, father of the Green Revolution in agriculture in the twentieth century.

- Sara Blakely, founder of Spanx, maker of bestselling undergarments for women.

Noticeably absent from this list: Steve Jobs, Bill Gates, Jeff Bezos, etc. While we admire each of them, too many other people use them as examples to learn from. Diversity in your stimuli matters!

Don't overthink the list—we drew this one up in about seven minutes (and yeah . . . we're geeks). Get some helpful background—don't assume that everyone will know a lot about each (hey . . . Curse of Knowledge alert!). Pick one at random. Free-associate about that person first—facts, accomplishments, anything you associate with them, their overall vibe/tonality . . . anything. This is not a test. And this is certainly not about the most immediately obvious connection you can make.

Back to greater sensory benefit from shower curtain rings. If you picked the Positive Deviance folks, you might jot down the following:

- Nonlinear results.

- Helpful variety, maybe even beneficial random variety.

- Limited range of movement, either physically or conceptually.

- Positive benefit where I'm not really expecting to see it.

- Dealing effectively with bureaucracy (the NGO thing).

You could then link back some of these associations to the sensory potential for shower curtain rings and start to get some of the following hatchling ideas:

- "Limited range of movement." This gets me thinking that the first ring travels the farthest when I pull the curtain. What different composition could it have to give you some sensory delivery? Maybe some synergistic effect in aroma. What all is true about that lead ring, or what *could be true* about it? Use that.

- "Helpful variety." Each ring could be colored and smell like a different plant in an English garden. The cumulative effect is really pleasant and rounds out a great total sensory experience.

- "Positive benefit where I'm not expecting it." The ring farthest out from entry often barely moves, if at all. Maybe it can be tugged to produce a soothing sound when you want it. Maybe there's some other role it could play.

- Heck, the idea of different roles for different rings is an entirely new idea to me, and I think I could generate a lot around just this!

The link between the mentor and the idea is not as direct it might have been if you chose Sara Blakely and proposed "Spanx material used in shower rings," but you could drive further out using her characteristics, her insight, and her innovative moves as stimuli to force-jump your own mental tracks. If you had chosen Larry Page (cofounder of Google) as your mentor, you wouldn't just work out a snazzy deal for shower curtain rings using Google Wallet. Go one or two levels of abstraction out from your example person to open up lots of fresh stimuli to link back to your task at hand. Again, use the earliest ideas as vehicles to push you out even further into entirely new territory. Who knew that shower curtain rings could make such a difference?

By the way, the Hedy Lamarr story is fantastic—a leading woman in film in the late 1930s through 1950s, and torpedo guidance-systems inventor in her spare time. Her work is incorporated into WiFi and Bluetooth technologies today.

The Strange Case of Skunk Baxter

Want to go even further in stretching out perspectives to get well beyond Confirmation Bias? How about "Top Weapons-Systems Consultant by day, Lead Guitarist for Famous Rock Band by Night?"

Meet Skunk Baxter, former lead guitarist from Steely Dan and the Doobie Brothers. This story from *The Wall Street Journal* shows how to get truly unexpected benefit from the least likely sources.[4]

> Mr. Baxter, who is now 56 years old, has gone from a rock career that brought him eight platinum records to a spot in the small constellation of consultants paid to help both policy makers and defense contractors better understand the way terrorists think and plan attacks. The guitarist-turned-defense-consultant does regular work for the Department of Defense and the nation's intelligence community, chairs a congressional advisory board on missile defense, and has lucrative consulting contracts with companies like Science Applications International Corp., Northrop Grumman Corp., and General Atomics Aeronautical Systems Inc.
>
> He says he is in increasing demand for his unconventional views of counterterrorism.
>
> "We thought turntables were for playing records until rappers began to use them as instruments, and we thought airplanes were for carrying passengers until terrorists realized they could be used as missiles," says Mr. Baxter, who sports a ponytail and handlebar mustache. "My big thing is to look at existing technologies and try to see other ways they can be used,

which happens in music all the time and happens to be what terrorists are incredibly good at."

One of Mr. Baxter's clients—General Atomics' vice president Mike Campbell—likens him to a "gluon," a term drawn from quantum physics that refers to the particles binding together the basic building blocks of all matter. Contractors and policy-makers say Mr. Baxter can see past bureaucratic boundaries and integrate information drawn from a variety of sources, though some who have worked with him say he can also be a self-promoter.

Mr. Baxter can speak the acronym-heavy vernacular of the professional defense consultant, but he would never be mis-taken for one of the hardened ex-military men who fill the ranks of the industry. He rarely wears ties, is fond of self-deprecating jokes, makes frequent popular-culture references, and peppers his speech with casual profanity.

. . . His defense work began in the 1980s, when it occurred to him that much of the hardware and software being developed for military use, like data-compression algorithms and large-capacity storage devices, could also be used for recording music. Mr. Baxter's next-door neighbor, a retired engineer who worked on the Pentagon's Sidewinder missile program, bought him a subscription to an aviation magazine, and he was soon reading a range of military-related publications.

Mr. Baxter began wondering whether existing military sys-tems could be adapted to meet future threats they weren't designed to address, a heretical concept for most defense think-ers. In his spare time, he wrote a five-page paper on a primitive Tandy computer that proposed converting the military's Aegis program, a ship-based antiplane system, into a rudimentary missile-defense system. On a whim, he gave the paper to a friend from California, Republican Rep. Dana Rohrabacher. To Mr. Baxter's surprise, the congressman took it seriously, and the idea proved to be prescient: Aegis missile-defense systems have done well in tests, and the Navy says it will equip at least one ship with the antimissile system by the end of the year.

"Skunk really blew my mind with that report," Mr. Rohrabacher says. "He was talking over my head half the time, and the fact that he was a rock star who had basically learned it all on his own was mind-boggling."

The evolutionary term "exaptation" applies here—taking an existing structure to see how else it could be used. An outsider's depth of knowledge in an entirely different industry helps him get past the "thought inertia" that insiders can't avoid. You can't get too tripped up by Confirmation Bias if you don't have a huge body of cherished beliefs to confirm. So reach out to people with other perspectives, or use your imagination to role-play with an unlikely mentor.

Confirmation Bias in Concept Development and Testing

The sport of fishing provides a useful metaphor for Ideation, Concept Development, and Testing. You increase your odds of finding fish if you cover more territory. It's generally not too productive to assume the fish will be wherever you happen to anchor your boat. Cast your line as far as you can in Ideation, and then very slowly reel it back through Concept Development. Let consumers tell you how far is too far. Deliberately extend the range of concepts to find those spaces where you're more likely to get full-on bites—hook, line, and sinker. That's unlikely to happen if you just dangle your line over the edge of your boat. The rush to solution will defeat the purpose of the kind of innovative thinking that supports the development of proprietary knowledge.

Questions To Ask when Testing a Concept Portfolio

- In addition to those areas we know we need to consider, what entirely new spaces could we cover in the portfolio so we can learn things that no one else in the industry is thinking about?

- Are our concept portfolio and learning plan broad enough, or are they too redundant and confirming of our cherished biases and unexamined assumptions?

- How can we test our assumptions about how to do things right in our product-market space? What deliberately disconfirmatory stimuli can we put in just to see what happens?

- What are the "weak signals" that others might be ignoring? How can we tune our attention to ideas that might not be immediately productive, but could form the basis for Relevance further out, or point to a new path we could be taking sooner?

- How unique is our take on where the industry is going? How can we start having thoughts that have never occurred to our competitors?

The greatest value in any given customer space has yet to be discovered. That's worth repeating. *The greatest value in any given customer space has yet to be discovered.* Someone will get there first, whether it's you, your current competitors, or an entirely new entrant. By going farther out in perceptual space to set up richer conversations during Concept Testing, you can more easily find out what's "too far," what's "too close," and what's "just right." Sometimes going way out there with provocative concepts can take you to a value of 100 along a particular benefit-delivery line when the industry is stuck on 35 and doesn't even recognize the additional range. While 100 may be too far for current customers, 65 might be a game-changing win. Working incrementally up from current offerings—the fishing-just-over-the-boat's-side approach might only get us to 40 or 45, leaving much open room but still providing the Uniqueness needed to get attention.

Things to Do to Overcome Confirmation Bias:

- Do some Assumption Busting. Especially the assumptions that are in play right at this point. Go "meta" for just a moment. List these assumptions, even the ones so obvious it's almost hard to call them out. Your competitors probably haven't done this in a very long time. Hold them only as assumptions, not inviolable laws of nature. Get clear on what you want to transcend. For autos, assumptions are as simple as "it must have four wheels and a steering wheel," or they are used to transport humans. Even "closer in" things might be: must make the passengers comfortable in the ways we all know, must allow sitting, etc. It's easy to come up with a lot of hidden assumptions quickly, some leading to more fantastical places if you violate the assumption, others leading to something closer-in. A useful rule of thumb would be: "Strong assumptions, loosely held." Just being aware of these assumptions will give you the necessary space to view them as nothing more or less than they actually are—assumptions.

- Remember to think of concepts as learning vehicles, not launch candidates. View the portfolio of concepts you developed and test them as very specific vehicles for learning. You can take a top-down or bottom-up approach.

  ○ Top-down approach starting with a specific learning need you have, and then developing a specific concept vehicle to test and find out more in that area. After getting a much better sense of where you could play from Ideation, ask yourself what you most need to learn. Like the *Moneyball* premise, focus on searching for new proprietary value that others don't view as vital. (See box.) Remember, you're not flying blind here. You heard possibilities in Ideation that could be formulated into learning opportunities. Start making a prioritized list. Then get ruthless and focus on what's most strategically advantageous to learn. Cut the "nice to learn" from this list of "absolutely, positively must learn." Per *Moneyball*, look for learning that doesn't just reiterate the industry's conventional wisdom.

  ○ Bottom-up approach from a concept you really want to test tied back to the learning need that it will satisfy. If you need to get right at it, make sure that each concept isn't just being thrown in to see how it does, but to learn at least one important new thing, and not just "Does that concept work?" The concepts are much more valuable here as Learning Vehicles than Launch Candidates. Make the concepts earn their spot to get on the list. Avoid including a concept when it is driven by one person's pet area (even if it's someone really important, if you can realistically avoid spending a valuable concept "slot" on it). If an idea won't help you learn something new, ask yourself why it should bump out of the list another concept that could.

Westin's Heavenly Bed[5]

Don't rest on your laurels—rest on a comfy bed while you're away from home.

While Westin Hotels may have worded their objective differently, the message is the same. In 1999, Westin transformed the hotel industry with the introduction of the "Heavenly Bed." Before that innovative move, hotels focused on upping their entertainment amenities. Westin took a different approach and went back to hotel basics by focusing on giving guests the best sleep they could get away from home. They did this by creating the Heavenly Bed. From its snowy-white duvet to its plushy, pillow-top mattress, Westin found a niche to own that made so much sense in hindsight that it seemed too simple to work. And yet, not only did every hotel chain—from budget to upscale—follow suit, it also gave Westin Hotels a new revenue stream. People wanted to have that "best sleep they could get away from home" at home. This opened up more opportunities for Westin—including Heavenly Bedding, Heavenly Baths, and Heavenly Spas.

9

Framing—
Like a Fish in Water

"There ain't no dark until something shines."
—Townes Van Zandt

IN ONE OF THE MORE MOVING COMMENCEMENT ADDRESSES YOU WILL find, David Foster Wallace tees up our dilemma:

"There are these two young fish swimming along and they happen to meet an older fish swimming the other way, who nods at them and says, 'Morning, boys. How's the water?' And the two young fish swim on for a bit, and then eventually one of them looks over at the other and goes, 'What the hell is water?'"[1]

We often aren't aware of the host of decisions previously made by others that put together the lens through which we view everything. We can't not think in terms of frames, or the way things are presented to us (acknowledging that there are, indeed, alternative ways to present them).

We understand relatively, not absolutely. All perception is based on context. Quick question—What's the legal drinking age in most of the United States? Hold that thought. We'll come back to that question in just a moment.

Have you seen this before?

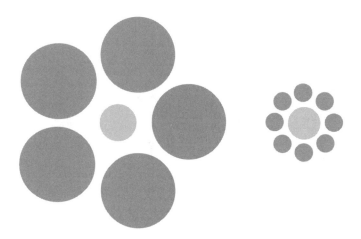

How much larger is the lighter circle on the right than the lighter circle on the left? Write your guess here if you have a pen handy: _____ or on a notepad if you're reading this in e-book form. Seriously, please, play along!

It's actually the same size (and yes, we verified it because even knowing the answer here didn't persuade our eyes!). And if you guessed 20 percent larger, then we also tricked you a little by getting you to think of something close to that number when we asked about the drinking age. Context, even if unrelated, can impact our response to what follows after.[2]

As humans, we can't avoid understanding everything through its context. We need a frame in order to understand what's inside it.

A dollar is a dollar is a dollar. And it's always worth exactly one dollar. Unless it's framed as a *discount* or a *surcharge*. Context makes all the difference. Research shows that a dollar paid as a *surcharge* is actually seen as a larger amount than a dollar gained as a *discount*. Well aware of this effect, the credit card industry lobbied to ensure that any difference between paying cash and using a credit card would take the form of a "cash discount" rather than a credit card "surcharge." A *surcharge* on credit card use sounds like a penalty to cardholders, while a discount is a bonus to those using cash.[3] Remember, losses loom larger than gains in our mind. A lost dollar has a bigger impact on us than a dollar gained. Nope, not rational, but real.

Now, valuing a life seems a bit crass. We'd like to think we would be especially careful about calculating the value of a life. But again, context can mix things up. We actually value life differently when we consider "saving a life" vs. "preventing the loss of a life." When presented with options to *save* a life that involved saving a set number for sure or taking a gamble on saving a larger number, test subjects opted for the sure thing; however, they were willing to gamble when the situation was recast as *preventing the loss of life*. As Daniel Kahneman noted in *Thinking, Fast and Slow*: "System 1 . . . is rarely indifferent to emotional words: mortality is bad, survival is good, and 90% survival sounds encouraging whereas 10% mortality is frightening."[4] The odds are the same either way, but the context of "survival" or "mortality" makes all the difference. This same line of research went on to demonstrate that "even highly trained physicians are susceptible to these effects and make different decisions depending on how the odds are framed—further evidence that yes, even doctors are human.

And the effect of framing becomes even larger when you add the social element. It is demonstrated every day that eyewitnesses can be "led" by the language used to ask them about what they saw. The witnesses of a car accident dramatically increased their estimate of the speed of the car when they were asked how fast the cars were going "when they *smashed* into each other" versus "when they *hit* each other."[5] Are we really that susceptible to framing? Yep. We really are.

So why is the influence of framing so powerful? As with each of the Cognitive Biases we have been examining, framing serves an adaptive function. Our brains are constantly bombarded by an endless stream of stimuli—more than we can possibly take in and process (without walking off the sidewalk into traffic). Framing provides a mental/perceptual filter that helps us make the most efficient use of the flood of information we are facing every second. And the filter serves two important functions: (1) it draws our attention to the thoughts and perceptions that make it through the filter we are employing in a particular context and (2) it blocks out information that our unconscious mind deems unnecessary or irrelevant, often without the benefit of our more sophisticated conscious mind. So the choices we make, the actions we take, are all guided by, and subject to, the mental frame that operates outside of our awareness.

Here's the process behind framing:

1. We always view the world through a certain lens, called a "frame" in psychology.

2. That lens is imposed automatically by our nonconscious mind and is shaped by our experience and the context we are in.

3. We are unaware that we are seeing the world through a filter and believe that we are seeing the objective truth. It is difficult to remove or change the lens because it is nonconscious and we don't even realize it's there!

4. It is important to acknowledge that the frame is there in the first place as an initial step to shifting frames.

5. Once we acknowledge that we are using a certain frame, we can remove the lens and try other frames—reframe the problem.

6. Reframing the problem can lead to a fresh perspective, which in turn leads to unique and relevant insights we otherwise wouldn't have had because we were seeing only a particular slice of the world, and not all that there was to see.

Imagine the official tour a head of state is given when visiting a totalitarian regime. What he or she sees is undoubtedly true *as far as it goes*, but the framing is clear. The whole picture will not be presented. Nothing whiffing of a problem or concern makes the cut. That's what we're often presented with daily, even when the presenter isn't quite as calculating as Team Jong Il. We ourselves have made our share of PR moves to put the most advantageous frame around our message, often nonconsciously. It's that human thing again.

Framing in Opportunity ID

Einstein was quoted as saying that if he had an hour to solve a problem, he'd spend the first fifty-five minutes figuring out the best question to ask and then solve the problem in just five minutes. We too often ignore the power of framing our challenges better. While we might not go to Einstein's extreme—such hyperbole may be an effective way to illustrate a point, but it's rarely a wise course of action—we certainly can avoid the mistake of solving a lesser problem or assuming too quickly that the problem is stated in the best way to think of it.

Consider the following ways of framing the same "statement of purpose" for an idea-generation session:

1. How to sell our excess stock of ping-pong balls?

2. How to get rid of lots of tiny, feather-light balls?

While the first statement of purpose seems perfectly reasonable, and the second seems rather odd, the first statement already presumes that we will be selling ping-pong balls through our current channels, to our current customers, in the same way we always have. Ironically, it was our unconscious framing of the task that made this sentence sound so reasonable, and inadvertently limited the possibilities.

The second purpose statement broadens the frame to include other distribution channels, other customers, other uses for the "feather-light balls" and even alternatives to selling the balls. The possibilities are intriguing, as they should be.

There are assumptions behind how we frame everything, from our most important decisions to the casual observations we make as we travel through our world. Sometimes the assumptions are so deeply buried we can't even imagine other ways of framing our thinking. In his enlightening TED Talk "Weird, Or Just Different?" Derek Sivers contrasts how the people of Japan name the blocks of their cities and consider the streets to be "just the unnamed spaces between the blocks." Sivers explains, "Sometimes we need to go to the opposite side of the world to discover the assumptions that we didn't even know we had, and realize the opposite of them may also be true." He goes on to point out that there are doctors in China who are paid to keep patients healthy, not merely to treat illness. While this may sound like "prevention" from our modern, Western frame of reference, the traditional Chinese approach to medicine actually had people pay their doctors for the months that they were well and not pay them when they were sick. Weird, different, or really smart? It depends on our frame of reference. The Chinese must think it is odd that our doctors are paid as long as we are sick and we stop paying them when we get well. From their perspective, there could be a conflict of interest in that arrangement.

Back to the early part of the innovation process. You need to do some significant work in framing your challenge or opportunity in a way that will lead you in a new direction. If you frame it just like anyone else in your category, you've already ceded the first big opportunity to create the Uniqueness you will need to be innovative. And if you frame it exactly the way you've always framed it in the past, you're likely to come up with the same old ideas that you've come up with before.

The Creative Problem Solving model suggests that we diverge at key stages to consider a few different possibilities, then converge and select the ones we want to move forward. Most people typically think of diverging only around ideas or solutions, but fail to think about generating multiple options for the problem statement itself. Finding the right articulation for your purpose on a given innovation initiative really matters—you'll seek what you set yourselves up to seek, and you'll find what you set yourselves up to find. So the time and effort spent on really examining and shifting how you frame the challenge will be well spent.

For example, you might see a big opportunity "To generate new ideas for convenient products in category X." The traditional approach would be to consider that a perfectly functional Project Purpose and move on to the "real work" of making that happen. Now consider a few different ways of teeing up that big opportunity:

- To generate new product ideas in category X that dramatically increase the entire end-to-end product experience, from selection to reuse.

- To increase convenience for users of category-X products through new products *or* new services, new product-services bundles, etc.

- To establish our brand as the leader in *Smart Convenience* for category X through new products, services, breakthrough consumer engagement, communication, and other new offerings.

- To exploit Brand Y's acknowledged brand equity for _____ to create entirely new approaches to increase convenience within category X.

- To create an entirely new subcategory within category X focused on those consumers who will pay a premium for dramatically more convenient products.

See how each of these purposes will guide you in a different direction? Yes, it's all about convenience, but some of these statements will clearly help you create the Uniqueness and Relevance you need better than some of the others. Some of these approaches might work better for innovation within an established brand, while others might work better for entirely new-to-the-company or new-to-the-world products. Regardless, the additional detail is not to limit possibilities, but actually to expand the richness of where you could play.

And further, you need to consider that you might not be asking a broad enough question here. Why *convenience*? What's going on in the customer's life that points to more convenience or new types of convenience? Are they especially time-crunched when it comes to the typical usage occasion for products in your category? What assumptions have you already made that keep it within that frame? What if you could relax some of those key assumptions? What if you made something else a bigger issue than convenience?

Maybe your customers are focusing on convenience because they have already made assumptions that limit what they believe would be feasible. Do they want more convenience *only because* they think they can't get what they really want? Do they even know what they really want? Convenience is often a secondary benefit, but may be a "cost of entry" to a larger customer consideration set that they have not yet imagined. "More-convenient hot sandwiches for lunch" is a different game than "Keep me satisfied and delight my senses within the twenty minutes I have available for lunch." Satisfaction and sensory delight might be what you need to go after, not convenience. Customers may limit their desires because they think the best they can hope for is a decent sandwich in the limited time they have for lunch. But what if they could have both a convenient-enough meal and a sensory experience that is more than they could have hoped for during a twenty-minute lunch break? Suddenly greater convenience becomes much less relevant. That's framing!

Opportunity ID (and Ideation) cannot happen in a vacuum—you're starting with something, so make the most of what you're starting with. What noteworthy things does your company or brand already get credit for? If you went away, what would people miss most? Is that overall broad opportunity area exploited fully? What bets have you already made on the future and how can you come up with congruent innovations to keep driving on these bets?

It is equally important to frame the problem in a way that gets people excited and enthusiastic about meeting that challenge in unexpected ways. You want it to have some edge, some inherent interest, some energy—even in the way the problem is stated. In other words, make it a little sexier! Think about it as the difference between Yawn and Yeah! Here are some objectives that raise the game:

Yawn: How to reduce employee absenteeism?

YEAH! How to keep every employee engaged so they're excited to come to work?

Yawn: How to encourage customers to start saving money prior to the usual triggers of getting married or having a baby?

YEAH! How to make saving sexy to singles?

Yawn: How might we create new laundry detergents that will steal share from the competition?

YEAH! How might we transform doing laundry from being a chore to being a pleasure?

Two of our favorite tools to help clients reframe challenge statements are *Word Salad* and *Abstract or Concrete*. Both of these tools will help you "try on" many different articulations of your challenge statement so you can determine which one will lead you to new, relevant, productive ideas.

Word Salad

Word Salad is an approach to forming a stronger innovation purpose statement. We will be using a simple example as an illustration, but know that this tool will work equally well with more complex problems.

1. Write your challenge statement as you currently see it. For example: "How might we improve the relationship with our largest customer?" Your statement should have each of the following elements:

- A problem-solving starter phrase: "How might . . . "

- A problem owner: "we"

- A verb: "improve"

- An object: "the relationship with our largest client."

2. Now, select either the owner, the verb, or the object. Work on one element at a time. For our example, we have chosen the verb—"improve."

3. Create a long list of alternative verbs that could replace "improve" in your challenge statement. Be sure to consider some words that are stronger and others that are milder, some words that mean exactly the same thing and others that mean something slightly different. Even consider words that mean the exact opposite. In our previous example, we changed the idea of "reducing absenteeism" into the idea of "engaging employees." Using a word that meant the opposite helped us to come up with a more provocative challenge statement.

   The goal here is to discover a new way of looking at the challenge, to help you come up with new ideas for solutions that you haven't thought of before. It is best to create a long list of potential substitutes—as many as you can think of. Do not fall into the trap of judging or analyzing the value of each one as you go. Just create a very long list, with no assessment. The analysis and decision making will come later.

   Substitutes for the verb "improve" might include:
   - Enhance
   - Amp up
   - Build

- Recreate
- Destroy
- Rebuild
- Create an entirely new . . .
- Maintain
- Patch
- Revitalize
- Grow
- Broaden
- Expand
- Limit
- Position for future growth
- Change the perception of
- Forge stronger
- Partner more closely
- Ensure

4. Now create a long list of potential words or phrases that you could substitute for the "object" in our challenge statement (in bold): "How might we improve **the relationship with our largest customer?**"

   How might we improve . . .
   - Sales to our largest clients?
   - Our dependence on our largest client?
   - Partnerships with our largest client?

5. You can do the same with the problem owner if you think it could be framed differently or that others might be able to influence the issue in some way. In this example, you might consider "our customer" as the problem owner in some of the restated problem statements.

Once you have the lists of potential substitutes for all the elements of the problem statement, you can begin combining them in different ways to create new statements. As before, try to make as many combinations as possible. You may have to modify some words to make the different elements go together smoothly, but this is part of the process. You are likely to think of new substitutions as you go. The *Word Salad* technique is extremely productive throughout the entire process. Since we didn't experiment with different owners of the challenge, the following examples represent possible combinations of endings for the following stem.

How might we:

- Change our customers' perception of us as a single-item supplier?
- Truly become a trusted partner for our largest customer?
- Limit our dependence on our largest customer?
- Insure ourselves against a reduction in sales to our largest customer?
- Amp up our proactive sales efforts with our largest customer?
- Leverage our relationship with our largest customer to start supplying their other divisions?

• • •

Sometimes one of the substitutes will spark an entirely new chain of thinking that may result in changing another part of the challenge statement. For example, the word "limit" made us think of a new object: "our client's perceived need to have a stable of three different suppliers of the items we offer." Thus, we might create a new challenge statement of "How might we limit our customers' perceived need to have multiple suppliers of our goods?" As you can see, the ideas that would be generated from this challenge statement would be quite different from those that would come from the original challenge statement, "How might we improve the relationship with our largest client?"

The objective of this tool is to help reframe the problem or challenge in a way that will lead to new ideas. The key to success is considering many varied potential problem statements, and then selecting the one (or ones) that are going to lead the team in the most productive direction. In our experience, when a team takes the time to work through this process, they almost always end up in a new and different place, with much more potential for innovation.

When the challenge statement is really nailed in a way that sets up a new paradigm, the process of generating new ideas for solutions flows surprisingly easily. Most people think that the "newness" in the problem-solving process comes only during the idea- or solution-generating phase. We find that there can be as much or more newness prompted by good work on the challenge statement. A provocative challenge statement, by its very nature, produces new thinking and new solutions.

Abstract or Concrete

Abstract or Concrete is another useful tool to help reframe a challenge statement to be more productive in sparking new ideas. It is more time-consuming and a little more challenging to execute than *Word Salad*, but it is incredibly powerful. It works particularly well for multifaceted challenges, or challenges that have many different stakeholders who may see the problem a bit differently. This technique can also be effective if you are working alone on a challenge statement, but it is particularly useful when a group needs to agree on a challenge statement. You need to plan the appropriate amount of time when using this tool with a group—this is certainly not a fifteen-minute exercise. Depending on the group size and the complexity of the challenge, it might take an hour or two, or even a whole day for a knotty problem.

One of the side benefits of this tool is that it will likely spark new thinking, and discussions will arise that haven't occurred before. So you need to plan in enough time for those discussions to bear fruit. And you also need to be watchful that the time is being used wisely, so you will have to facilitate the group carefully to allow space for discussion and still keep the focus and the momentum. If you need to work on a complex challenge, you will want to consider hiring a professional facilitator to manage the process.

This tool works by helping you view the problem or challenge at different levels of abstraction—for example, when you want to examine different ways to state the challenge in language that's more concrete or more abstract. This is often useful when it feels like the problem is really broad, or conversely, when the problem seems really narrow. (We often refer to a problem statement that's too narrow as "dancing on the head of a pin.") If your challenge statement is so narrow that it simply doesn't leave room for new ideas, then you need to broaden it by making it more abstract. If your problem statement is so broad that you don't even know how to begin, then you likely need to make it narrower. And if it's a really complex problem, it may actually have several facets, some narrow and some abstract, that you will need to tackle in order to solve for the entire thing. This tool will help you tease out whether you are working at the right level of abstraction.

To use an analogy from healthcare, this might be described as determining if you are attempting to eliminate a symptom instead of curing the underlying disease. But it can also help you determine if you are attempting to cure an underlying disease without first controlling the most urgent symptoms that might risk the patient's life and must be treated before the underlying disease can be addressed. You can certainly lose the customer before you get to unveil your big solution if you don't first address their more urgent needs. This tool helps you identify the most appropriate level of abstraction for your work. And you might even discover new facets of the problem that you might not have identified if you hadn't examined your challenge statement in this way.

1. Begin with your challenge statement as you see it now. Again, we're going to use a very simple example for this illustration, but keep in mind that this tool works exceptionally well for complex problems. In fact, it's best used on complex problems; simple problems probably don't require the time and effort that this powerful tool will require.

    Let's pretend my friend Jay thinks he needs a new car. As a good friend who's interested in his emotional and financial wellbeing, I've decided to help him tease out if that's really the "problem" he needs to solve. So I begin by asking him some questions to help him articulate what the real problem or need might be. We begin with a problem-solving statement in the same form as the example from *Word Salad*.

    How to get Jay a new car?
    - Starter phrase = How to . . .
    - Verb = Get.
    - Problem Owner = Jay.
    - Object = New Car.

2. Next, begin asking questions that will result in problems statements that are more and less abstract.

- "Why is that important?"

- "Why does that matter?"

- "What would happen if you did that?"

3. When an answer is given, rephrase that answer into a "How to . . . " problem statement. For example, when we asked Jay why it's important he get a new car, he said it's because he's starting to have expensive repair bills on his current car. We rephrase that answer as *"How to reduce repair costs?"*

    - We asked him why else (other reasons) it is important to get a new car. He replied that he's bored with his current car. We again restated that as *"How to reduce Jay's boredom?"*

    - You can push these answers and resulting challenge statements to even more abstract statements by asking, *"Why is that important?"* in response to the most recent answer. When I asked Jay why it's important to reduce his boredom, he responded that he just needs a little more excitement in his life.

    - Again, we restated the answer into a problem-solving statement: *"How to add some excitement to Jay's life?"*

It's probably becoming obvious that getting a new car might be only one potential solution for adding excitement to Jay's life, if that's the real problem. But buying a new car is a fairly costly proposition. What if that problem could be solved by something as simple as buying a new TV? Or learning a new sport? Or planning a fly-fishing vacation? By really digging further into the current perception of the problem, we may find new, better, or more cost-effective solutions to the real problem.

4. Continue to ask the "Why is that important?" or "What would happen if you did that?" questions to draw out a variety of *different* responses.

   • Be sure to rephrase *every answer* into a problem-solving statement. For some, you will want to push even further to more abstract answers by asking why the previous answer is important. The goal is to get to a large variety of possible answers, and thus a large variety of possible challenge statements.

   When facilitating this process with a group, be sure to elicit answers from everyone in the group. If one or a few people dominate the discussion, you run the risk of not uncovering all the important aspects of the problem. People bring different lenses to every problem based on their expertise, their life experience, their role as related to the issue—their frame of reference. If you're working on a problem that's meaty enough and you decided it's worth the time to take a group through this process, then it's worth ensuring that all perspectives are heard.

5. Once you (or more importantly, the group) decides that you have covered a broad range of more abstract challenge statements, it's time to begin asking different questions that will drive downward to more concrete problem statements.

   • Begin asking, "How might that be accomplished?" or "What's stopping you (or us)?" As before, continue to put "How to . . ." in front of each answer to rephrase that answer as a potential problem statement. As before, you can drive further into even more concrete statements by asking the same question about the previous answer and resulting challenge statement.

6. Now that you have a wide variety of both more abstract and more concrete problem statements, it's time to begin prioritizing them. It's possible your team will have an aha moment and realize that one possible problem statement has "nailed it," but it's more likely that you will need to have some solid discussion on the pros and cons of several of them. Many teams realize they need to work on several problem statements, and perhaps in a particular order, to solve the overarching problem. So, as we indicated when we introduced this tool, be sure to plan enough time for these deeper discussions.

In our work, we call those multiple problems statements Target Areas. You might also label them Platforms, or Opportunity Areas, or White Spaces, if you're working in New Product Development. Whatever label you give them, be sure to capture them. And, yes, as you might now be fearing, you should play with lots of different ways of teeing up each of them to come up with the best articulation of that particular Target Area.

When you have well-defined, differentiating Target Areas that go beyond everyone else in the category, you're already building momentum for innovation. Conversely, if you frame the problem the same way as everyone else, then you have already lost an important opportunity. Your company should have a different take on any broad opportunity area. Establish an empowering context for these Target Areas. Think of the Who/What/When/Where/Why/How around an opportunity area and then sketch in just enough detail to get your Ideation participants on the same launch pad. This isn't to "lead the witness" or give them the answer, but to pull together helpful understanding so there's enough "there" there that folks can start cranking out original ideas and solutions.

TO GO UP, ASK:

"Why?"
or
"Why does that
matter?"
or
"What would happen
if you did that?"

LADDER
OF
ABSTRACTION

TO GO DOWN, ASK:

"How?"
or
"What's stopping
you?"

Rephrase as, "How to get Jay a new car?"

SUMMARY

Ensures you're working on the right "level"
of the issue (or the right issue).

- Should you be working on a more
  abstract version or a less abstract
  version of the challenge statement?

Helps especially when stated problem is very
broad or very narrow.

You may discover that the real "problem" isn't
what you initially thought.

- What you initially thought was the
  problem may simply be one potential
  solution for the real problem.

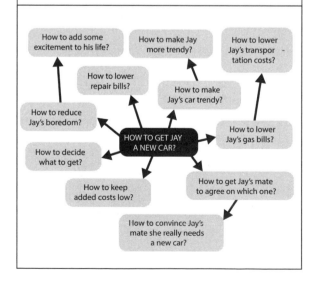

Framing in Ideation

For the Ideation session, getting your Purpose Statement to the right place helps. Setting up Target Areas that already have energy is essential. Now it's time to explore opportunities to frame the process in ways that drive your Ideation into the magic zone of Uniqueness and Relevance.

Worlds Excursion. Framing up some key part of the Target Area in an entirely different context of experience can be really helpful to drive us well beyond the obvious. For example, imagine we're working on new-product possibilities for umbrellas and the Target Area is "Quantum-Leap Possibilities for Umbrella Versatility." Let's play with that. With this excursion, we send pairs or trios to dramatically different contexts to look for elements of Versatility there. The idea is to get us past our individual, immediate, proximate (and unconscious) definitions of Versatility and to see how we can expand our thinking about it in different areas.

So, we might send one pair to the "world" of cuisine, another to music, another to sports, and yet another to science fiction. The idea isn't to generate versatile-umbrella ideas that are food-related, or directly related to any of the contexts, but to see how considering Versatility within cuisine gets us thinking about very different ways that Versatility could intersect with new-umbrella possibilities.

So, let's try this out. What's versatile in cuisine?

- Immediately, we think of a Cuisinart® food processor and its multiple blades, bowls, etc. We think of the storage system to keep all those options organized and easy to access. So let's jot down some of this as stimuli, and try not to be overly literal with it (e.g., a new umbrella handle onto which I can pop other umbrellas with different diameters, or add extensions to the circumference). Instead, go even further out. Extracting the *principles* here will be more generative than directly borrowing ideas.

- Another thing—we might try a quick Google search on "versatile kitchen innovation" and find things like a new chef's sauté station that both cools and heats. So the principles here could be extra benefits from the umbrella for differing temperature conditions, or even more broadly, an umbrella that covers the extremes of use from children to the elderly. Again, we're just playing with the places the stimuli can take us.

- One more—one of us might remember a favorite cutting board, the Joseph® Joseph folding cutting board (please do Google it if you're not familiar with it) that has a folding handle and grooves underscored on the bottom side of the board. When you're done cutting, you grab the handle and the sides of the board come up so you can pour what you just chopped into the frying pan or mixing bowl for your next steps. The principle we can extract from this excursion is *sequence*—what's something that happens right before or right after normal umbrella use?

And that was just from cuisine! If we were doing this, my partner and I now could probably generate a dozen new versatile possibilities for umbrellas. And the other pairs are finding new ways of thinking about this Target Area in their assigned "worlds" that will each generate a dozen or so ideas.

Framing in Concept Development

We have two tools here to keep our framing of the concepts on track—*Insights* and *Language Temperature and Balance*. We want to make sure the concept is expressed as compellingly as possible—great ideas deserve great expression. It's sad when poorly constructed concept language takes down a really great idea.

Fresh, Resonant Insights. Back to the building blocks we discussed earlier in chapter 3. The Insight establishes the frame for the concept. It answers *why* a concept would be compelling. It's not limited to the problem the concept will solve with its Benefit—it's more about what's in the customer's mind that sets the stage for the concept Benefit to matter powerfully to the customer, and then for the Product Description and other "Reasons to Believe" to clinch the deal.

We're trying to evoke a "spontaneous head nod" from the target audience. We want to understand where they're coming from and we want them to understand that we've been there and done "this" to take them to a whole new level of satisfaction. Again, the Holy Grail here is *obvious only in hindsight,* which contains the two things we're looking for—Uniqueness and Relevance.

Conversely, things to avoid include the following:

- Reverse Benefits masquerading as Insights—"Gee, wouldn't it be great if you had . . . " or "Customers want . . . ." Why would it be great or why do customers want it? Think of the sentence right before these types of Insight wannabes. We're trying to connect to a deeper level of understanding and the "why" behind the want is really important, not just for communication, but to help us "stick the landing" on the product itself. Will it really pay off with what the Insight gives us?

- Category Homilies—Save the homilies for fine needlepoint work. We need new Insights that set you up for proprietary advantage. Common category starting points have little or no chance of helping you drive to Uniqueness. The freshness dating is past expiration on most of these stale insights.

- Research Findings—These might start pointing us toward building out great Insights, but they're just building blocks. We need to understand the emotion and the context. The Insight can be based on a research finding, but it must be much more than just that. Research findings alone will never get a spontaneous head-nod from your target customer.

Language Temperature and Balance. We had a great experience working on establishing the right language "lexicon" for an entirely new product category a few years back. The clients needed to understand the best way to set up this new category through communications that extended beyond the positioning of any one product within the category. We asked ourselves which perspectives might be especially helpful for this project and brought in a semiotician—a professor adept at meaning making and symbols. We asked her to help us understand the territory our *Creative Consumers* associates were constructing with the language possibilities they were generating. Her perspective was invaluable in helping us understand language "temperature" more concretely—a lot of the language fleshed out a "warm-cool" communications spectrum vs. a "hot-cold" range. But we also considered this metaphorically, as we then recognized that thinking in terms of "temperature" was helpful in raising our awareness of the intensity of other variables.

We noticed *balance* as an important way to understand the potential for communicating effectively here, similar to John Naisbitt's "High Tech/High Touch" formulation of years back. One example: the language communicating product efficacy in this new category had to be balanced with a sense of nurturing and care. It wasn't about overpowering the customer, but effectively helping the customer feel really well cared-for while dealing with a particular issue they were facing. Going too far in either the "strength" or "nurturing" direction was not going to get us where we needed to be.

It is particularly important for innovation professionals to remind themselves that *framing* is always occurring. We either become consciously aware of our frame of reference, the frame of our colleagues, participants and customers, or allow those influences to limit our possibilities. We need to be frequently reminded that we tend to see the world through the frames and filters that we have developed naturally and unconsciously over the years. We generally accept the frames that we are presented with by others who may not have our interests in mind.

By using some of the techniques that have been presented in this chapter, you can expand the frame to bring Uniqueness and Relevance to whatever challenge you accept.

10

Steps Forward

"Everything is overdetermined."

—Sigmund Freud

FREUD BELIEVED THAT DREAMS ARE TRIGGERED BY MULTIPLE FACTORS in the life of the dreamer—from recent, random, minor events to deep traumas and wishes buried in the subconscious mind. He coined the term "overdetermined" to describe how one condition is created by many seemingly divergent influences. But isn't everything overdetermined?

History is rarely as clean as the linear account we are given in high school history class. Our need to assume tidy cause-and-effect patterns regularly draws us to the simple explanation. Many of us are fans of Occam's Razor—the hypothesis that the explanation requiring the fewest assumptions is usually the correct one.

Cognitive biases don't usually come wrapped up as clean, hermetically sealed phenomena the way we've laid them out in each chapter. We regularly see a great deal of overlap and interplay between the different Cognitive Biases. Just as certain illnesses have their "comorbidities"—for example, diabetes and cardiovascular disease—Cognitive Biases do show up in clusters.

A great example of how Cognitive Biases don't work alone comes from one of our team members who worked at a well-known small electric appliance company and saw a perfect storm of the Curse of Knowledge, Confirmation Bias, and Status Quo Bias, all spinning simultaneously. Here is her story:

> We had done some good "opportunity discovery" work about white spaces in the category. One opportunity area we discovered was in the water filtration category. Clean water is a huge need globally, and at the time, there were no *electric* water filters available other than complex, expensive, and difficult-to-maintain reverse osmosis systems. The most common water filtration systems available used either gravity feed (like a Brita® pitcher) or water pressure from the tap (like the Pur® faucet-mount system). Each of the existing solutions failed to adequately address the consumer problems, either due to cost, effectiveness, or ease of use. So there was a clear need for a better solution.
>
> One of the prevailing corporate strategies was to shift a percentage of the business toward global markets. The need for convenient, effective, and affordable water filtration is far more urgent outside the United States, since tap water in the US is generally safe to drink (in the US, most people buy water filtration devices for better-tasting water, not for safer water). In many other countries, tap water is not safe to drink, so nearly every home has some sort of water filtration system to make the water drinkable. With the consumer need and corporate strategy very much aligned, a project was born.

Small appliances turn very slowly—people buy only one iron every twenty years. So in this business, manufacturers make money by having a specific profit margin on each unit and essentially never going under that. This is a category "given." In contrast, water filter manufacturers make very little money on the sale of the unit itself. They count on a high repeat purchase of the very profitable refill cartridges.

As we were developing this product, I used this perspective to advocate for having a very low margin on the unit, with a high margin on the refills, but everyone else insisted that we make a high margin on the unit. I happened to be the person with the least time in the small appliance industry; I had come to the company from another industry. So I didn't have the same Curse of Knowledge about the small appliance business as everyone else on the team. I had been doing all my research on the water filtration business and had a different fund of knowledge to apply to the business model. However, everyone else on the team, and all the senior executives, had a lot more experience in the small appliance industry, and they simply could not wrap their minds around this other business model; it was simply too foreign and too contrary to all the data they collected and all the experience they had.

I was forced by senior management to price the unit at what I knew was an impossibly high price. Their assumptions were: (1) it would be sold in the small appliance aisles in stores, alongside all the other appliances that use the same business model; (2) it would be bought by the same buyers who buy other small appliances and expect the same price-points; and (3) it was highly unique, and thus could command a high price. I told them in every meeting that I believed their pricing model was wrong. At one point, the VP of Marketing said to me "You have brought this up at every meeting. We have heard you. We don't agree with you. I don't ever want to hear this from you again." At that point, I had to give it up and develop the product with their high margin model.

When it came time to launch the product and sell it in to the retailers, I was vindicated. We sold—none. Not one single unit. All the retailers said the price was far too high for the unit, and they wouldn't stock the refills because they wouldn't sell enough units to turn the stock.

Needless to say, the project died a quick death and was never rekindled. This was really a shame, because we had an excellent product that solved all of the problems with existing solutions. It could have been a great business, all around the world. But Cognitive Biases killed it.

Beyond the specific remedies to each Cognitive Bias that we have laid out throughout the book, there are some general reminders that will help deal with Cognitive Biases in innovation. We're in this together—in our susceptibility to Cognitive Biases and our efforts to lessen their impact.

We ask you to keep three important things in mind as you move forward to address the tricky combinations of Cognitive Biases you'll encounter. They are timeless, straightforward, and are all-effective in combatting the negative results of multiple Cognitive Biases: humility, curiosity, and a spirit of play.

1. **Stay Humble.**

   As Fred Kofman notes, "Ontological arrogance is the claim that things are the way you see them, that your truth is the only truth. It is the belief that the only valid perspective is the one you hold, and that anybody who sees things differently is mistaken. The ontological arrogant (ontology is the branch of philosophy that asks what actually exists) does not distinguish his personal opinions from objective truth; for him, his opinions are the truth. Neither does he distinguish his subjective experience from objective reality; for him, his experience defines reality."[1]

Let humility keep you honest. No one of us has the complete picture, ever. At best, we can aspire to have a better partial picture than others might possess. We've established that we all succumb to Cognitive Biases, so nurture that nagging suspicion that you just might be slanting things your way—you are, we all are, because we can't help it. Plus, staying humble is just good human capital. Strong people can afford to be humble while still pushing for better results. It's inspiring to see leaders say "I don't know" when they really don't. We want our leaders to lead, *and* we want them to be human.

Humility will help you with the following biases in particular:

- Negativity Bias—You know that negativity appears profound and somehow more responsible. You also know how you can unwittingly use negativity to your advantage by making ideas you don't like appear foolhardy or untested. But we have also shown how you can extract value from even the most outlandish ideas if you will allow yourself to entertain them (and be entertained by them). Let humility give you the space to play and to get the most out of every idea.

- Availability Bias—Relying on that "What you see is all there is" isn't enough. You now understand how incomplete your archive of quickly retrieved memory is. Maintaining your humility will encourage you to seek out more stimuli to add to the mix, providing more perspectives to consider.

- Confirmation Bias—"Business is about action, right? We already know where we landed on that issue—let's go!" Humility can help you keep Confirmation Bias from taking over, especially when a premature rush to solution prevents you from investing your innovation with all the Uniqueness and Relevance necessary to win. Keep pushing! When early decisions are necessary, don't let them be carved in stone. You'll know when it's time to lock things down for the sake of a successful launch. Until then, hold your early decisions loosely. Consider them to be the best you knew at the time, and be ready to add or revise as new information becomes available. Curse of Knowledge—you are not your target consumer, even if you look a lot like your target in terms of demographics, psychographics, media usage, and purchase behavior. You aren't your target because, try as you might, you cannot put yourself fully back in their shoes regarding your products. You eat, sleep, and dream your category. The target doesn't. You have likely "assumed away" more prior knowledge about your category than most of your target audience will ever have. Stay humble, stay thirsty, my friends. Keep wrestling with better and better ways of understanding your customers' predicaments, knowing that you'll never fully get there; but honor their patronage by continually trying.

2. **Keep Curious.**

In his pitch to the BBC for the popular, long-running quiz show QI, producer John Lloyd laid out the big "Why?" for the show—"There is nothing more important or more strange than curiosity . . . We share with our primate cousins three basic drives:

food, sex, and shelter. But humans possess something else: a fourth drive. Pure curiosity is unique to human beings. When animals snuffle around in bushes, it's because they're looking for the three other things. It's only people, as far as we know, who look up at the stars and wonder what they are."[2]

The great news about curiosity is that it's as innate as the Cognitive Biases. Our default mode isn't *only* skewed to the problematic. We all share the drive to figure out our world. According to Prospect-Refuge Theory from art and architecture, when viewing landscapes, people from all cultures prefer viewing natural landscapes that promise both safety (refuge) *and* mystery or opportunity (prospect). We all prefer something that promises novel areas to explore while also providing a sense of safety.[3]

Why is curiosity such a compelling drive? The individuals of millennia past who got to stick around long enough to pass on their DNA were more likely to be those who balanced curiosity and its acquisition of new knowledge with self-preservation by sticking to the tried and true. Our neurology evolved to associate curiosity with pleasure. We all get that—there's a thrill to learning and trying something new. Part of our brain gets a pleasant hit of dopamine when we learn something new, eat great food, or enjoy sex. Connecting curiosity's payoffs with the pathways already established for our most primal pleasures—smart move, evolution!

Apparently this fourth drive of curiosity is not evenly distributed. Some of us want to go directly from point A to point B and get right to the answer, while others want to do a little exploring on side roads en route. It's not so much about how curious you are as it is about how you're curious. Becoming more curious in your preferred way will yield benefits.

The best innovationistas and marketers that we have met do not ever assume that they *know* their consumer absolutely. The best ones are very *curious* about their consumer all the time.

- What is changing now that _____ is happening in the marketplace?

- Why are they doing what they are doing?

- What else do they need?

- How do they feel about this change that we have made?

- What is the underlying need that is driving this new trend?

- How do they like to be talked to about this?

The key is *curiosity*.

Don't use your research and experience as a holy knowledge base that can never be questioned. That research is only as good as the purpose for which it was commissioned, at the time it was conducted. All research based on need and preference has a shelf life.

In instilling a culture of innovation, you need to be a consumer adventurer. You should be exploring the rich landscape of consumer understanding to find new, uncharted territory. That metaphor can be stretched in several ways:

- You need to be ready for anything—be open for threats, delights, and unexpected turns in the road.

- You need to be humble—this is not your native land. Be ready to challenge what you already understand.

- It is a journey, not a destination. No matter how many products you have launched, you are still not "done." You need to keep learning and exploring.

Curiosity will help you counteract the following biases:

- Confirmation Bias—What if the core assumptions of our industry are beginning to lose their Relevance? What assumptions are we making that are so baked into the recipe that it's difficult even to pull them out? Curiosity coupled with a little healthy paranoia is a good thing.

- Framing—Simply asking "What if we looked at this another way . . . ?" can be powerful. Recognizing that you are always framing your thinking in ways that are outside of your awareness gives you the opportunity to challenge your own assumptions and try other ways. Change the frame, change the game.

- Conformity Bias—Group cohesion can be a beautiful thing, but not in and of itself. Be curious together. Forces of conformity are often anti-curiosity, which can lead you to a strained and often premature surety and away from the opportunity to do something meaningfully different for your customers. Be together in ambiguity for just enough time to consolidate the sturdy learning as it comes, and move on to the next field of opportunity and inquiry.

3. **Never let the light of play extinguish from your eyes.**

   One thing we do share with many other mammals is the need for play. We somehow talk ourselves out of it as we become fully functioning adults, and that actually works against us.

   Scientists across the physical/natural/social spectrum see play as a meaningful biological process. The reward pathways for food, sex, and—as we just established—curiosity are reprised through play. Play increases fitness for survival in many animal species, as it makes participants smarter and more adaptable. For humans, as with our unique gift of curiosity, it elevates our sights and increases empathy, which innovationistas can always appreciate.

Mental play in particular is important for innovationistas. Grim determination is only required at very specific points throughout the innovation process. Successful innovation occasionally requires the power to walk through walls, but mental play is necessary far beyond its obvious role in Ideation. We need to bring the spirit of play into almost every stage of the development process. Play catalyzes. Play synthesizes. And play creates emotional energy and resilience.

Remember, we're looking for both Uniqueness and Relevance, and not merely in the definition of the new products we create, but in the entire customer experience, in the marketing communications of our products, in launch, in the products' infancy in the marketplace, and as they grow up. Play drives Uniqueness in every step of bringing our baby to market.

As Stuart Brown and Christopher Vaughn observe, "There is a kind of magic in play. What might seem like a frivolous or even childish pursuit is ultimately beneficial. It's paradoxical that a little bit of 'nonproductive activity' can make one enormously more productive and invigorated. Play is the basis of all art, games, books, sports, movies, fashion, fun and wonder—in short, the basis of what we think of as civilization. It's what makes life lively."[4]

We have clearly learned on this journey through the various Cognitive Biases that we are highly irrational, emotional creatures . . . and so are our customers. You can tell when filmmakers love the films they produce, or when chefs love the dishes they've prepared, or when product developers love the products they put out. Play is love. Play is kicking things around more, getting beyond the obvious. Play brings in the heart to complement the terrific "head work" we do for a new product. We do need both.

With these characteristics in mind—humility, curiosity, and a spirit of play—move forward courageously. Awareness of the Cognitive Biases we discuss in this book and taking action on your increased understanding will make you not just more effective in your innovation efforts, but more effective in working with others overall, including coworkers, family, and friends.

11

Conclusion

"Know Thyself."

—Forecourt inscription at the Temple of Apollo at Delphi

TALL ORDER, THAT. THROUGHOUT THE BOOK, WE'VE EXPLORED THE largely nonconscious biases that give us scripts that we're predisposed to run. We need to unveil more of this nonconscious activity to start the valuable effort of knowing ourselves. It's not a one-and-done effort. But it's so interesting to get going on it!

Consider again that we're not just walking into a meeting with Sally from R&D, Tim from Finance, Hector from Manufacturing, and Georgette, our VP of Innovation. We're walking into that meeting with lead shoes, blinders, revisionist history, balloon ballast, unreliable eyewitnesses, an electric-fence collar, the fawning Emperor's retinue—and all of this while attempting to take in our official tour of a totalitarian state.

How does any good work ever get done? It's a tribute to our resourcefulness that all the extra baggage doesn't stop us from innovating. But it can be better.

We hope we've made the point that we can do something about it. Some of the key researchers in behavioral science aren't overly optimistic about our being able to get rid of these biases; but awareness of the biases, some understanding of their composition, and some vigilance about our disposition to succumb will make important, helpful differences in your work.

Remember that the biases discussed carry the force of thousands of generations. We are all predisposed to fall victim to them. They feel comfortable and cozy, even if we don't like where they lead us. Rooting them out entirely from the cognition we inherit won't happen in our lifetime, but watching for them and then taking quick action with simple tools helps. And we certainly can't do anything about them if we don't understand them.

Behavioral Innovation is innovation that goes in—into your head, into your daily work, into you. It's IN-novation. It will change you. You'll quickly start catching yourself before slipping into automatic behaviors and interpretations of what's happening. This will happen several times daily. It's funny. And humbling. Anyone getting on the BI path who assumes he or she is then operating from a position of being able to judge others will be missing the point—it's an ongoing, even endless, effort. But it's so rewarding. *We are all in this together.*

The tools of BI will have helpful carryover into your personal life outside work. It's helping you get a better overall OS on which you can run everything in your life.

Pick one or two of the following things to do *now* so you can begin your journey using the tools of Behavioral Innovation:

- Look for opportunity. Jot down right now a few places in your innovation efforts that seem to be operating the most on autopilot. What seems the most reflexive? Early on? Later? When a particular cast of characters is assembled more than when others are? What appears to run mostly on System 1's gut reaction?

- What part of your current process needs the most work? How could Behavioral Innovation change things up there? Think of helpful specifics vs. generalities. Make this more "available" to you later by making it vivid.

- Pick one small thing to do differently where you need the most work. Perhaps this is not the time to take on the biggest sacred-cow bias that is tripping you up. Just a small piece of it. Microresolutions (picking just one small thing to do differently) lead to microhabits (ingrained behaviors). Gather enough microhabits surrounding one opportunity and you're quickly making a dent in it.

- There are four main places you can scan to pin down the right opportunity:
  - Individual thoughts and beliefs.
  - Individual behavior.
  - Collective thoughts and beliefs, AKA culture, "the unwritten order of things," "how things are just done around here," etc.
  - Collective behavior, systems, processes—how groups of people, procedures, technologies, etc., actually behave.

Kick these around. You'll land the right opportunity.

For more tools, case studies, and audiovisual resources, head over to www.OutsmartYourInstincts.com, try something, and then come back and try something else. Then give us some feedback about how it's going for you.

We will be on the Behavioral Innovation journey for a long time, and are committed to your success within your BI journey. In the works, as of this writing in early 2016, are two additional books taking

Behavioral Innovation into additional areas for exploration and further development.

Thanks for joining us. Innovation is such a rewarding and fantastic way to invest your life's energy. For those of us who choose to spend more time at it . . . maybe we're just dopamine junkies, maybe we're just the annoying kindergarteners who never quit asking "why," maybe we're just the ones who were lucky enough to find a productive outlet for our quirks. Whatever—we salute you! We pledge our ongoing efforts to help you mow down obstacles of any kind and to strengthen your resolve to fight the good fight of innovation. Starting with the internal battles in our heads is an important first step. Innovation doesn't need to be so hard if we're aware and proactive. We are thrilled to further the learning from the Behavioral Revolution and do all we can to make innovation the deeply satisfying calling that we all hoped it would be.

Onward, proud innovationistas!

Acknowledgments

So much great work is going on in both innovation and behavioral science. The complete list of influences and direct contributors is impossibly long to capture. The authors thank the following people for their contributions:

For ongoing insight and creative fuel for our efforts in Behavioral Innovation, many, many thanks to our colleagues Christine Haskins, Susan Wandell, Cynthia Ryan, Shari Morwood, Greg Cobb, and Dina Pancoast, who ceaselessly up the game for our offerings and continuously bring solutions to Cognitive Biases in everything you do.

Special thanks go to our partner, Christine, for her continuous inspiration, and to Dina for all she's done to turn this material into an engaging training curriculum.

For belief, vision, and the gumption to help turn our early manic language casserole into a better reader experience, Liza Babcock and Jill Reiswig deserve special acknowledgment and high praise.

To the intrepid Book Campers, who dug in early and got some life-giving momentum going: Salute!

For his insight and willingness to jump into something with little to no idea what it was, or what it would be, Jim Orfe is to be especially commended.

To our support team here at Ideas To Go: Thank you for freeing up our Facilitators to do what they do best.

To our inspiring community of Creative Consumers associates, we thank you for continually raising the bar on how to end run some of the key Cognitive Biases, and for bringing your whole person to our work.

For indispensable contributions to telling this story more accurately and responsibly, a healthy round of applause goes to Victor Carlson and Margaret Gorlin. Your input helped us to think more clearly about the topic and to clarify communication. You also pointed us to opportunities we hadn't thought of in telling this story. You provided important checks on our own cognitive biases and shortcomings in our early drafts.

To the fantastic folks at Greenleaf: deep bows. Special thanks to Liz Brown, Hobbs Allison, Tyler LeBleu, Sally Garland, and Magdalene Thomas. We're thrilled to have joined forces with such a great team on this important work.

Lastly, we thank you for spending some time to kick this around in your own head. May your adventures in innovation be fulfilling. Life's too short not to enjoy our work, deeply.

• • •

From Adam Hansen—

To my coauthors, Beth Storz and Ed Harrington, and our partner, Christine Haskins: Thank you so very much for your unflagging enthusiasm for our work. Your friendship and example inspire me to do more and better.

To Norine, my wife and love: Your ongoing support and love mean everything to me.

To James, Beth, Alex, and Tom: Our family forays into creativity, and the ways you march soulfully into your individual paths, continue to inspire me. I love you all so much. To TJ and Josie, thank you for helping me stay focused on doing what I can to leave you a better world.

To my dear parents: You gave me wings. I miss you daily.

• • •

From Ed Harrington—

I would like to thank those who have offered inspiration, education, and support.

Fred Meyer is the genius behind the fundamental approach to promoting the innovative thinking and solutions that are the foundations that our work and writings are built on. Long before innovation was a catchword, he saw the excitement and opportunity of using a creative problem-solving model and truly impactful co-creation methodologies, including the simple notion that if you want a creative idea, you ask a consumer who is creative. My mentor.

Adam Hansen saw the connection between what Fred created and behavioral economics. It's brilliant and fitting and fulfills one of the criteria of a great idea. As soon as people hear it, their reaction is "But of course, why didn't I think of that?" My esteemed colleague.

Beth Storz, the president of Ideas To Go, leads with great thinking and care and really gets stuff done—like this book! My other esteemed colleague.

Professor Ravi Dhar, George Rogers Clark Professor of Management and Marketing, and director of the Center for Customer Insights, introduced me to behavioral economics and its many influences and applications. My teacher.

My brother Joe believed in me and was always there when I needed him. My hero.

My dad was an incredibly creative person, stuck to some degree in an uncreative world. What can you say about someone who had you build not just sand castles, but sand cities complete with irrigation channels and drip structures, and who invented a game called Hit the Kid with the Cat (stuffed toy, no kid harmed, lots of laughs)? My inspiration.

• • •

From Beth Storz—

To my darling husband, Shawn: Thank you for your unyielding support and love, which makes it possible for me to do this work every day.

To my boys, Cameron and Nathan, who probably don't realize the role they play: Thanks for being the amazing kids you are. You make so much possible for me just by being you.

To my parents, John and Amy, and my sister, Cheryl: You have always been positive enablers for me in all of life's pursuits.

To my partner, Christine Haskins: Thank you for continuous inspiration. I'm looking forward to what you do with the next one.

To Ed Harrington: Thank you for always supporting me personally since Day 1 and for challenging us to make this work our best work.

To Adam Hansen: You were the catalyst for this work and led the charge down this incredible path to Behavioral Innovation. It wouldn't have happened without you. And also—thanks for being my adopted brother.

Notes

Chapter 2

1. Roy F. Baumeister, et al., "Bad is Stronger Than Good," Review of General Psychology 2001. Vol. 5. No. 4. 323–370.

2. T. M. Amabile, "Brilliant but Cruel: Perceptions of Negative Evaluators," *Journal of Experimental Social Psychology* 19 (March 1983): 146–156.

3. Derek Penwell, *Crazy Farming* episode of the DBCC Blog Podcast, July 15, 2014. Reference begins at the 6:47 time mark.

4. Amabile, "Brilliant but Cruel," 146–156.

5. Jennifer S. Mueller, Shimul Melwani, and Jack A. Goncalo, "The Bias Against Creativity: Why People Desire but Reject Creative Ideas," *Psychological Science* 23 (January 2012): 13–17.

6. "David Alger's First 10 Rules of Improv," http://improvencyclopedia.org/references/David_Alger%60s_First_10_Rules_of_Improv.html.

Chapter 3

1. Daniel Kahneman, *Thinking, Fast and Slow* (New York: Farrar, Straus and Giroux, 2011), 129–130.

2. Phil McKinney, web article, http://philmckinney.com/archives/2012/04/can-you-teach-yourself-to-avoid-doing-the-obvious.html.

3. Kahneman, *Thinking, Fast and Slow.*

4. Stephen Shapiro, http://stephenshapiro.com/best-practices-are-stupid/

5. *Enabling Manufacturers to Compete in the Global Economy*, 2010 Georgia Manufacturing Survey, Georgia Tech, Kennesaw State University and Habif, Arogati and Wynne, LLP.

6. David Aaker, *Brand Relevance: Making Competitors Irrelevant* (San Francisco: Jossey-Bass, 2011), 120.

7. Po Bronson and Ashley Merryman, "The Creativity Crisis," *Newsweek*, July 10, 2010.

Chapter 4

1. Explained by Edward de Bono in the 1960s as the ability to solve problems creatively or through an indirect route.

2. Chip and Dan Heath, *Made to Stick: Why Some Ideas Survive and Others Die* (New York: Random House, 2007), 19.

3. Miriam Rich, Virginia Tech, "Curse of Knowledge" presentation, https://www.youtube.com/watch?v=_DyC0fd395Y.

Chapter 5

1. *The Bias Against Creativity: Why People Desire But Reject Creative Ideas*, Muller, Melwani, and Goncalo, Cornell Digital Commons, January 1, 2011, http://digitalcommons.ilr.cornell.edu/cgi/viewcontent.cgi?article=1457&context=articles.

2. John Hagel III, John Seely Brown, and Lang Davison, *The Power of Pull: How Small Moves, Smartly Made, Can Set Big Things in Motion* (New York: Basic Books, 2012).

Chapter 6

1. Michael S. Gazzaniga, *Who's in Charge? Free Will and the Science of the Brain* (New York: Ecco, 2011), 75.

2. David MacLean, *The Answer to the Riddle Is Me: A Memoir of Amnesia* (New York: Houghton Mifflin Harcourt, 2014), 11–27.

3. Gazzaniga, *Who's in Charge?*, 77.

4. Jonathan Haidt, *The Happiness Hypothesis* (New York: Basic Books, 2006).

5. David Wolman, "The Split Brain: A Tale of Two Halves," *Nature*, March 14, 2012, http://www.nature.com/news/the-split-brain-a-tale-of-two-halves-1.10213.

6. Gazzaniga, *Who's in Charge?*, 85.

Chapter 7

1. Susan Bailey and Mairead Dolan, *Adolescent Forensic Psychiatry* (Boca Raton, FL: CRC Press, 2004), 73.

2. See website: http://ethicsunwrapped.utexas.edu/video/conformity-bias.

3. John Stuart Mill, *On Liberty* (London: Longman, Roberts & Green, 1869; Modern Library Ed., 2002).

4. Brandeis's concurring opinion in the Supreme Court Case *Whitney v. California*, 274 U.S. 357 (1927). Italics added.

5. Kurt Lewin, *Resolving Social Conflicts: Selected Papers on Group Dynamics* (New York: Harper and Brothers, 1948), 201-216

6. For quotes from Charles Munger, see *Poor Charlie's Almanack: The Wit and Wisdom of Charles T. Munger, Expanded Third Edition* (Marceline, MO: Walsworth, 2005).

7. Alex F. Osborn, *Applied imagination, 3rd ed.* (New York: Scribner, 1963).

8. Bruce Reinig and Robert O. Briggs, "On the Relationship Between Idea-Quantity and Idea-Quality During Ideation," *Springer Science and Business Media*, April 18, 2008.

9. Charlan J. Nemeth and Brendan Nemeth-Brown, "Better Than Individuals? The Potential Benefits of Dissent and Diversity for Group Creativity," in *Group Creativity: Innovation Through Collaboration*, (New York: Oxford University Press, 2003).

10. Jerry B. Harvey, *The Abilene Paradox: The Management of Agreement* (San Francisco: Jossey-Bass, 1988).

11. Denise Caruso, *The Whole Earth Catalog*, Summer 2001, http://www.wholeearth.com/issue/2105/article/110/hybrid.vigor.

12. Stephen Covey's Habit 6 from *The Seven Habits of Highly Successful People* is *"synergize,"* which he developed further in his book *The Third Alternative*.

Chapter 8

1. Margit E. Oswald and Stefan Grojean, "Confirmation Bias," in *Cognitive Illusions,* edited by Rudiger F. Pohl. Reprint Edition. (Florence, KY: Psychology Press, 2012), 79–80. Reference to Wason (1960), "On the failure to eliminate hypothesis in a conceptual task," *Quarterly Journal of Experimental Psychology,* 20:3 (1968): 273–281.

2. Paul Kedrosky, "History and Contingency," in *What Should We Be Worried About: Real Scenarios that Keep Scientists Up at Night.* John Brockman, ed. (New York: Harper Perennial, 2014), 442–444.

3. Reference to creative tension model comes from Peter M. Senge, *The Fifth Discipline: The Art and Science of the Learning Organization* (New York: Doubleday, 1990), 139.

4. Yochi J. Dreazen, "Rocker Jeff Baxter Moves and Shakes in National Security—Once With Doobie Brothers, Now in Counterterrorism, He Has Ear of Pentagon," *The Wall Street Journal,* May 24, 2005.

5. http://usatoday30.usatoday.com/travel/hotels/2009-05-14-westin-heavenly-bed_N.htm).

Chapter 9

1. Transcription of the 2005 Kenyon Commencement Address, May 21, 2005, http://web.ics.purdue.edu/~drkelly/DFWKenyonAddress2005.pdf.

2. Shane Frederick, *Thinking, Fast and Slow* presentation, Center for Customer Insights at Yale School of Management, Customer Insight Conference 2014, https://www.youtube.com/watch?v=6S2zHAcXk74.

3. Richard Thaler, "Toward A Positive Theory Of Consumer Choice," *Journal of Economic Behavior and Organization* 1 (1980): 3960.

4. Kahneman, *Thinking, Fast and Slow,* 367.

5. E. F. Loftus and J. C. Palmer, "Reconstruction of automobile destruction: An example of the interaction between language and memory," *Journal of Verbal Learning and Verbal Behavior,* 13 (1974): 585–589.

Chapter 10

1. Fred Kofman, *Conscious Business: How to Build Value through Values* (Louisville, CO: Sounds True, 2013), 22. http://www.axialent.com/pdf/Conscious%20Business%20by%20Fred%20Kofman%20-%20Ch%201%20English.pdf p. 22.

2. Ian Leslie, *Curious: The Desire to Know and Why Your Future Depends On It* (New York: Basic Books, 2014), xiv.

3. Ibid. Page 14.

4. Stuart Brown and Christopher Vaughn, *Play: How It Shapes the Brain, Opens the Imagination, and Invigorates the Soul* (New York: Avery/Penguin, 2010), 4–11.

Self-Assessment and Activity Guide

After reading each chapter, use the following questions to help you reflect on the concepts introduced. Then try the activities—or come back to them when you feel that a refresher course on the ideas in this book would improve your innovation skills.

Chapter 1: Introduction

Self-Assessment Questions:

1. When do you rely on the faster System 1 thinking, and when do you use the slower, more deliberate System 2 type? Can you think back to a time when you should have employed System 1 or System 2 more?

2. Consider the eight Cognitive Biases that have become part of our evolutionary fabric of life. When did one of those biases help you make a good decision? When did one lead you to the wrong decision or outcome?

Activities:

Make a list that includes all eight of the Cognitive Biases: Negativity Bias; Availability Bias; Curse of Knowledge; Status Quo Bias; Confabulation; Conformity Bias; Confirmation Bias; and Framing.

1. Think of a product that has had a successful introduction into the market—as small as an iPod, or as big as a Tesla—and note how each of the biases may have been used to argue against the product's success. If it's easier, come up with the argument, and then see which of the biases it fits into. For example, for the iPod, Availability Bias may have argued that people wouldn't want to be forced to use iTunes—a program that many PC users were not familiar with. Or perhaps Status Quo Bias argued that users prefer exterior buttons, rather than the innovative clicking wheel.

2. Can you come up with more arguments that may have surfaced against the iPod? How about in favor of the iPod? Or think of another breakthrough product that seemed like a long shot when it was introduced. What biases might the innovators have had to resist?

3. Now consider an idea that's been simmering in the back of your mind. Write it down. (Don't be afraid—this is a brainstorming session. There are no right or wrong answers!) Test your idea; in what way might it be a real winner? How might it fail? Now examine your answers in light of those pre-programmed Cognitive Biases that can seem impossible to shake off. Are any of the reasons for "failure" merely biases in disguise? If you could rid your idea of the shackles of those biases, could it be a success?

Chapter 2:
Negativity Bias—Bad Is Stronger than Good

Self-Assessment Questions:

1. How often do you fall victim to Negativity Bias—either in your own thinking, or in someone else's? How does it make you feel? Millennia of evolutionary forces have trained us to avoid looking stupid in front of others. How often do you avoid voicing creative ideas for fear of being thought foolish, impractical, or just plain odd? Can you think of innovators who pushed ahead with their unusual ideas? What would it take for you to have the courage to push through the resistance in your own and others' minds?

2. Think of a time you quashed your own or someone else's idea with the knee-jerk response: "Yes, but . . ." Bring the idea back and, while silencing your nay-saying voice, give the idea a little more consideration. Can you imagine a bit of merit in the idea? Is it difficult to shut off your negative bias? Can you get better with practice?

Activities:

1. Choose an object, any object—a chair, a kite, an apple—and imagine turning it into something new. You can do this alone, or in a group. Throw out ideas about how to reconstruct the object. The rules here—as outlined in Chapter Two—are that every idea gets added to with the words "yes, and . . ." You might find yourself with a really inedible apple, but some of the ideas may spark new ideas that warm up your brain for future idea-generating sessions.

2. You may have completed the author's "Forness" exercises in this chapter. Here's your chance to do them again. Choose a new idea for a product, process, or artistic endeavor. Draw a large "T" on the page, and on the upper left, write "for," and on the upper right, the words "wish for." Now fill out the "for" column with ideas that appeal to you about the object. If you're considering something like condos that rotate like a Ferris wheel, perhaps in the "for" column you'd write: "Give every resident a penthouse view." Now, in the "wish for" column, list issues that need to be addressed. Start your list with "I wish for . . ." or "How might we . . . ?" For the rotating condos, you might write "How might we make it structurally sound?"

3. Do the exercise again with a new idea. Practice, practice, practice! Recognize that deliberately coming up with a "bad" idea early on can help us get to much better ideas if we value the bad idea for its power to get us thinking of things we never would have considered otherwise.

Chapter 3:
Availability Bias—
What You See Is All There Is

Self-Assessment Question:

Role-playing, or pretending, is an excellent way to get out of your head—out of the habits of Availability Bias that restrict us to what we already know. To let creative ideas flow, it often helps to change our approach, even our scenery. Have you ever looked at a problem from a new point of view and been surprised by all you could see?

Activities:

1. Consider a problem that makes you feel stuck—something you've puzzled over for a while. Now imagine you're looking at the problem from the top of a cold mountain in New Hampshire. How about on Waikiki Beach? You might even try a real change of scenery—go to a museum, or a stationery store. Does a new setting help you see the problem in a different way? Do facets of the puzzle become clearer?

2. Find another problem you want to work on. This time pretend you're someone else—a mail carrier; an architect; a busy mother; a ninety-year-old grandparent; a nine-year-old soccer player who's always sitting on the bench. What kinds of needs, desires, and goals do you have when you become someone else? How might this help you break past Availability Bias to new solutions?

Chapter 4:
The Curse of Knowledge—
Well, It's Just Obvious that . . .

Self-Assessment Questions:

The Curse of Knowledge often gets in the way of innovation—acting as an "unconscious guardrail"—by assuming away the hard, early work we had to go through to get to our expertise, taking for granted the facts we internalized long ago. Have you felt these limits preventing you from fully understanding what your customers might struggle with? Your struggle now may be to explain something to someone who doesn't have the background knowledge you do. What helped you reverse the Curse of Knowledge and dismantle your unconscious assumptions?

Activities:

1. Let's do some assumption-busting. Start with a new idea for a product you'd like to create within your current business. Complete the following:

   a) In our business, everyone knows _____ .

   b) We have to _____ .

   c) Our product is/does/has _____ .

   d) Of course we always _____ .

   e) We make/sell _____ .

   f) We do _____ by _____ .

   Now think again about that new product idea, and go through this list again. Ask yourself: "What if this is not/were not true?" or "What if it weren't entirely true/untrue?" Does this give your new product idea more space to become something?

2. Think of several assumptions you hold about your market and your customers. For each assumption, ask yourself, "What if that is not true?" Can you feel this let in some light and perhaps propel you forward in your push to innovate? Even if there are compelling reasons for the assumptions, being able to ask "What if . . . ?" about them will take you to helpful places to play with new, better ideas.

Chapter 5:
Status Quo Bias—The Bird in the Hand

Self-Assessment Questions:

1. As we attempt to innovate, the option of not doing anything is always on the table. It's often the most alluring, comfortable choice; but it can also be the most harmful. Do you tend to cling to the status quo, and resist change? Why do you think that is? Is it based on past experiences with change being painful? Or is it something less tangible—perhaps simply fear of the unknown, which is often where change takes us?

2. Can you remember a time in your personal life when making a change seemed like the scariest thing imaginable—but now you're glad you did it? Where would you be if you hadn't ever changed in your _____ years on earth? What forces are keeping you tethered to the status quo? How does it feel if you let go, just a little?

Activities:

1. Holding onto the status quo is like keeping so much ballast—weight—in your hot-air balloon that you remain earthbound. Consider an idea you've been knocking around in your head—a new product, service, or approach to a task. Make a list of the reasons it feels comfortable not to move forward with this idea—a list including the ways in which maintaining the status quo feels like the easiest and most comfortable action. Now go down that list and cross off each reason, one by one, and imagine yourself casting off weights holding down your idea-balloon. Can you feel yourself getting lighter? Are you able to reach a higher altitude, a new vantage point, and thus see a different horizon?

2. Risks of Omission describe the things we miss out on by not pushing ourselves into new territory. Think back to a decision you made to not act. What were some of the positive outcomes you missed out on? What were some of the negative ones you avoided?

Chapter 6:
Confabulation—
Of Course That's Why I Did That!

Self-Assessment Questions:

1. How much do you confabulate (nonconsciously lie) to yourself about your motives, beliefs, or actions? Are you aware when you do it? What happens when you slow down and watch yourself— rather than jump to unquestioned conclusions?

2. What happens when you slow down and really listen to others, rather than assume you know their intentions?

Activities:

1. Choose an activity or product you've wanted to pursue, but haven't because of what you assumed would be the disapproval of others. Create a dialogue (in your head or on paper) in which you let the other person explain her reasons to you; but when it's your turn, remain silent and let her keep speaking, and let her get to the deeper reasons for her beliefs. (If you need to "ask" questions to get deeper answers, feel free.) What new information did you glean regarding the other person's motives?

2. Now go try this exercise with a real person. Try to remain silent, or when appropriate, probe the other person's ideas rather than rush to justify your own. Really practice listening, and aiming for transparency. Does this give you a new view of the situation, product idea, or relationship?

Chapter 7:
Conformity Bias—Play Along to Get Along

Self-Assessment Questions:

1. Do you often find yourself agreeing with others—just because it's easier? Do you do this because it's easier than having to explain yourself? It's safer to be part of the crowd? You want people to like you? Often conforming when we don't really mean it damages our self-respect; have you experienced this?

2. How does it feel when you don't conform? Which do you tend to choose: fight, flight, or freeze? Can you think of a time when standing out from the crowd is actually better? What would it take for you to become more comfortable with being an outlier, or bucking the majority?

Activities:

1. Pretend you're not a conformist, but a thrill-seeking feather-ruffler. You arrive at the office and there waiting for you is Consensus Clem, whose job it is to keep the tribe (including you) safe; to do this, he must keep everyone thinking and acting in unison.

But today, instead of arguing with him, you listen. You even take notes, and later reflect on them until you actually understand his ideas. Now go through that list and come up with a counter-argument that could take the tribe in a new direction. Ask what, why, and how this can be achieved.

2. Choose a new product or process idea, and list twelve Assistors and twelve Resistors—these can include individuals, corporations, cultures, policies, beliefs, etc. Now narrow the twelve down to the top five. Engage your curiosity, and ask the who/what/when, etc., questions of them—really trying to understand their points of view. Get curious. Go beyond the obvious. What new ways of seeing does this provide? How could you strengthen the key Assistor and weaken the #1 Resistor?

Chapter 8:
Confirmation Bias—Just As I Thought!

Self-Assessment Questions:

We often see what we already believe is there. Can you think of a time when doing this proved harmful to you or your company? Have you found yourself more likely to revert to confirmation bias in some areas more than others? Why?

Activities:

1. Time to flex those questioning muscles! Find a scene involving people—a news photo, people outside your window, coworkers in the hallway—and briefly note what you know to be going on.

Now wipe the slate clean and ask yourself: What if everything I assumed was wrong? What if those teary eyes on the front page were not sorrow, but joy? What if the coworkers in the hallway weren't wasting company time, but were holding an ad-hoc brainstorming session that resulted in creating the Next Big Thing, poised to make your company millions?

2. Turn those questions to your market. What do you know about your customer? Now flip it, so what you "know" is only half right; or perhaps exactly the opposite is true. How does this free you up for innovation? How can you get comfortable with actively disconfirming some of your most closely held beliefs about your market?

Chapter 9:
Framing—Like a Fish in Water

Self-Assessment Questions:

1. We tend to see, or not see, according to the filters we've put in our sight lines. What are some of your filters that might distort or totally block reality? How might you become more conscious of your tendency to frame things?

2. What might you do to eliminate or lessen the impact of this framing, so you are more capable of seeing things as they really are?

Activity:

Take a situation that has been puzzling or bothering you. List the top five obstacles holding you back. One by one, go down the list and (1) identify the "frame" or "filter" that may be part of the obstacle and (2) reframe or remove the filter, and view the obstacle again. Has it shifted, or at least gained some room to shift, as you give it more thought?

Apply this reframing technique to any problem, and you'll be amazed how a shift in perspective can reveal a whole new world.

Chapter 10: Steps Forward

Self-Assessment Questions:

1. To combat the tenacity of the Cognitive Biases, the authors close with three imperatives: Stay humble, keep curious, and never lose the sense of play. Is one of these harder for you than the others? How might you work on it? How might you continue practicing the trait(s) that come more easily to you?

2. The authors also suggest being aware of how the Cognitive Biases will improve not just your innovation efforts, but also your personal relationships—with coworkers, family, and friends. Can you identify a thorny personal relationship that has been made worse by the biases each of you is holding?

Activity:

Make a list of five relationships in your life that could use some improvement—those with family, friends, coworkers, or perhaps even with yourself. Next to each one, name the top three reasons for discord. Identify which of the eight Cognitive Biases—more likely two or more— you are holding onto in this relationship. Now combat them one at a time until you get a glimpse of what that relationship could be without the baggage of biases. Do you feel a tiny bit lighter? Keep going. It's a gift you're giving yourself; you deserve it.

Chapter 11: Conclusion

Self-Assessment Questions:

1. How has reading this book changed your perspective on becoming the kind of innovationista you've wanted to be?

2. By becoming aware of hidden biases, and working to overcome them, how can you make the world a better place?

Activity:

Make a list of improvements you wish to see in your work and in your life. Narrow down to the top five in each. Now choose one item from each list—one small thing that needs the most work—and get started. One day at a time. Make a small change each day, and try this four days running—and soon you'll have a mini habit. Microresolutions (doing just one thing differently) lead to microhabits (ingrained behaviors). Set in motion enough microhabits around a problem, and you'll quickly make a dent in it.

Index

A

Abstract or Concrete tool, 176–182
action, lack of, 87–88
Active Knowledge Transfer, 52
Adjacent Experts, 150
after-action reviews, 88
Amabile, Teresa, 17–18
Ariely, Dan, 8
Asimov, Isaac, 43–44
Assistors, 131–134
Assumption Busting, 78–80, 159
automatic thinking. *See* System 1 (fast)
    thinking
Availability Bias, 9, 45–67
    in Concept Testing, 62–63
    in Development Phase, 63–67
    humility and, 193
    in Ideation, 58–62
    in Opportunity ID, 48–58
    self-assessment questions, 218–219

B

bad, as stronger than good.
    See Negativity Bias
"Bad is Stronger Than Good"
    (Baumeister), 15
balance of language, 186–187
balloon ballast metaphor, 90–91
banning part of status quo, 93–94
Baumeister, Roy F., 15
Baxter, Skunk, 155–157
Bayesian inference, 123–124
Behavioral Economics (BE), 8
Behavioral Innovation, tools of,
    202–204

Benefit Areas, 12
benefits, disguised as insights, 78
"The Bias Against Creativity", 19
big ideas, total number generated, 95
bird in hand. *See* Status Quo Bias
Blink (Gladwell), 7
body language, 123
Bounded Rationality, 7–8
Brandeis, Louis, 129
breaking rules, 143–145
Broad Opportunity Areas, 94–95
Brown, Stuart, 198
buyer's regret, 20

C

Carlson, Stephanie, 64
Caruso, Denise, 141
Category Crashing, 54
Chain of Associations, 60–62
Challenger Space Shuttle disaster
    example, 128
Chinese doctors example, 168–169
Cirque du Soleil example, 101
close-in ideas, 118
Cognitive Biases, 9–11. *See also*
    Availability Bias; Confabulation;
    Confirmation Bias; Conformity
    Bias; Curse of Knowledge;
    Framing; Negativity Bias; Status
    Quo Bias
    overlap and interplay between,
        189–190
    overview of, 2
    System 1 (fast) thinking and, 4–5
coherence, need for, 107

collar metaphor, 130
Collateral Costs, 86
Commission, Risks of, 88
commitment to ideas, increasing, 38–39
commoditization, 99
common ground, 132
Concept Development, 13
    Availability Bias in, 63–67
    Confabulation in, 119
    Confirmation Bias in, 157–161
    Conformity Bias in, 137–139
    Curse of Knowledge in, 82–84
    doubling number of ideas for, 95
    framing in, 184–187
    Negativity Bias in, 42–44
    Status Quo Bias in, 96–100
concept portfolio, questions to ask
    when testing, 158–159
Concept Testing
    Availability Bias in, 62–63
    Confabulation in, 120–124
    Confirmation Bias in, 157–161
    Conformity Bias in, 139–141
    Status Quo Bias in, 100–103
concrete. See Abstract or
    Concrete tool
Confabulation, 10, 105–124
    in Concept Development, 119
    in Concept Testing, 120–124
    in Ideation, 118–119
    in Opportunity Identification (ID),
        109–118
        creating environment of
        transparent observation,
        115–117
        giving rationalizing mind a break,
        112–115
        working with creatively bold
        consumers, 117–118
    self-assessment questions, 222–223
    System 1 (fast) thinking and, 107, 110
Confirmation Bias, 11, 143–161

in Concept Development and
    Testing, 157–161
curiosity and, 197–199
humility and, 194
in Ideation, 151–157
in Opportunity ID, 147–151
path dependence, 145–147
rules and, 143–144
self-assessment questions, 224–225
Conformity Bias, 10, 125–141
    in Concept Development, 137–139
    in Concept Testing, 139–141
    curiosity and, 197
    in Ideation, 134–137
    in Opportunity ID, 130–134
    self-assessment questions, 223–224
    System 1 (fast) thinking and, 126–127
    System 2 (slow) thinking and, 126–127
conscious thinking. See System 2 (slow)
    thinking
consensus. See Conformity Bias
consumers. See customers
context, perception based on, 164–165
costs, collateral, 86
Creative Consumers associates, 77
Creative Ethnography service, 52
Creative Problem Solving model,
    169–170
creative tension model, 149–150
creatively bold customers, 75, 117–118
creativity, biases against, 19, 96–97
"The Creativity Crisis" (Newsweek
    article), 65
curiosity, 83, 194–197
Curse of Knowledge, 9–10, 69–84
    and challenge of working with
        customers in innovation, 76–77
    Confirmation Bias and, 194
    in Development Phase, 82–84
    in Ideation, 78–82
    during Opportunity Identification,
        73–76

self-assessment questions, 219–220
customers
    asking questions to, 74–75, 99
    curiosity about, 83, 196–197
    deciding for, 43
    longitudinal involvement of, 83

D

Dalkon Shield contraceptive IUD
    example, 127
deciding for customers, 43
Deprivation technique, 93–94
development of concept. *See* Concept
    Development
differentiation, 22–24, 56
discount example, 164–165
disproving hypothesis, 145
"Diverse by Design," 49–50
doctors in China example, 168–169
dog's electric fence collar metaphor, 130
doing nothing, risk of, 87–88
DREAM (Delete-Reduce-Enhance-
    Add-Maintain) technique,
    100–101
driving forces, 131–134

E

easing entry into the new, 86
Einstein, Albert, 167
electric appliance example, 190–192
electric fence collar metaphor, 130
"The Emperor's New Clothes," 147
Endowment Effect, 86
exaptation, 157
Excursion Theory, 58–62, 64
expertise, 6–10, 150
extracted information, synthesizing,
    123–124

F

failure, fear of, 21
false negatives, 16

false positives, 16–17
falsifying hypothesis, 145
fear, 20, 21
fish in water metaphor, 163–164
fishing metaphor, 157–158
focus groups, 63. *See also*
    Conformity Bias
    discussion in, 120–123
    listening to without immediately
        interpreting, 115–117
    thoughtful laddering in, 115
Force Field model, 131–134
Ford, Henry, 100
forness thinking, 31–42, 59, 135
framing, 11, 163–187
    using Abstract or Concrete tool,
        176–182
    in Concept Development, 184–187
    curiosity and, 197
    in Ideation, 183–184
    in Opportunity ID, 167–172
    self-assessment questions, 225–226
    using Word Salad tool, 172–176
freedom of speech, 129
Freud, Sigmund, 189

G

gains vs. losses, 164–165
Gatorade, 89–90
Gazzaniga, Michael S., 105, 106–107,
    112–113
Get Fired, Get Hired technique, 92–93
Getting Real during Concept
    Development, 42
Gibson, William, 146
Gladwell, Malcolm, 7
goals, for Ideation, 94–95
grabber pickup tool, 97
graphics, Transient Hypofrontality and,
    114
groups. *See* focus groups
groupthink, 127–128

H

habits, small, 203
Haidt, Jonathan, 109
Hansen, Adam, 229
Harrington, Ed, 229–230
Heavenly Bed example, 161
heuristics, 7–8
Hightower, Jim, 125
hindsight, obvious only in, 48, 57, 115, 117, 118, 127
Hoffer, Eric, 85
humility, 192–194
hybrid vigor, 141
hypothesis, disproving, 145

I

iCoN® panelists, 77
Ideation, 12–13
    Availability Bias in, 58–62
    Broad Opportunity Areas, 95
    Confabulation in, 118–119
    Confirmation Bias in, 151–157
    Conformity Bias in, 134–137
    Creative Consumers associates and, 77
    Curse of Knowledge in, 78–82
    framing in, 183–184
    goals for, 94–95
    iCoN® panelists and, 77
    lateral-thinking customers and, 77
    Negativity Bias in, 24–34
    Status Quo Bias in, 92–96
    System 1 (fast) thinking during, 4
    Target Area for, 118–119
images, Transient Hypofrontality and, 114
improvisational theater, 40
inaction, 87–88
indispensability, 56
individual input, 120–123
individual learning vehicles, 43

innovation, stages of. See Concept Development; Ideation; Opportunity Identification (Opportunity ID)
Innovation Prevention, 130, 131–132
insecurity, 20
insights, 185–186
    defined, 57
    development of, 118–119
    mining of, 54
    reverse benefits disguised as, 78
internal interests, 91–92
Interpreter Module, 112–115

J

Japanese streets example, 168–169
Johari Window tool, 51–54

K

Kahneman, Daniel, 3, 16, 45, 165
Kawasaki, Guy, 133
Kay, Alan, 55
Kedrosky, Paul, 146
knowledge. See also Curse of Knowledge
    flows of vs. stocks of, 103
    sharing across boundaries, 52
Knowledge Journey, 51
Kodak, 88–89
Kofman, Fred, 192–193

L

Lamarr, Hedy, 154
lamppost metaphor, 124
language
    Abstract or Concrete tool, 176–182
    effect/influence of, 32–33, 165–166
    temperature and balance of, 186–187
    Word Salad tool, 172–176
lateral thinking, 76–77
learning vehicles, 43, 160
Lewin, Kurt, 131

life, value of, 165
literal thinking, 77
Live Takeout, 63
Lloyd, John, 194–195
losses vs. gains, 164–165

M

MacLean, David, 105–107
manual transmission example, 110–111
Marx, Groucho, 15
McKinney, Phil, 46–47
meaning, need for, 107
mental excursion, 58–62, 64
mental play, 198–199
metaphorical thinking, 59–62, 64
microhabits, 203
microresolutions, 203
Mill, John Stuart, 128
Moneyball (Lewis), 101–102
multiple perspectives, 147–151
Munger, Charlie, 132
muscle memory, 111–112

N

Need States, 12
Negativity Bias, 9, 15–44
    in Concept Development, 42–44
    deciding for customers, 43
    Forness® process and, 31–42
    humility and, 193
    in Ideation, 24–34
    in Opportunity ID, 22–24
    overview of, 2
    self-assessment questions, 217–218
    System 1 (fast) thinking and, 16, 25,
        36–37, 41
    System 2 (slow) thinking and, 36–37
Newton, Elizabeth, 71–72
nonconscious processes, 105–107. *See
    also* Confabulation
nothing, risk of doing, 87–88

O

obvious only in hindsight, 48, 57, 115,
    117, 118, 127
Occam's Razor, 189
Ogilvy, David, 124
Omission, Risk of, 87–88
On Liberty (Mill), 128
ontological arrogance, 192–193
Opportunity Areas, 181
Opportunity Expansion, 149
Opportunity Identification
    (Opportunity ID), 12, 202–203
    Availability Bias in, 48–58
    Confabulation in, 109–118
        creating environment of
            transparent observation,
            115–117
        giving rationalizing mind a break,
            112–115
        working with creatively bold
            consumers, 117–118
    Confirmation Bias in, 147–151
    Conformity Bias in, 130–134
    Curse of Knowledge during, 73–76
    defined, 48
    framing in, 167–172
    Negativity Bias in, 22–24
    Status Quo Bias in, 91–92
"overdetermined," 189

P

party planning exercise, 25–30
pattern-recognition system, 3–4
perfectionism, 20
perspectives, multiple, 147–151
ping-pong balls example, 168
Pinto example, 127
Platforms, 181
play, 197–199
playing along. *See* Conformity Bias
point of view (POV), 12, 23

post-hoc explanations, 106–107

postmortems, 88

prefrontal cortex (PFC), temporary
    suppression of, 114–115

pretending, 64, 66

product possibilities, total number
    generated, 95

Projection, Principle of, 114–115

Prospect-Refuge Theory, 195

proto-concepts, total number
    generated, 95

Q

questions, asking customers, 74–75

R

randomness, confronting Availability
    Bias using, 60–62

Rational Actor, 7–8

rationality. *See* Bounded Rationality

rationalization. *See* Confabulation

Reason To Believe language, 78

reflective thinking. *See* System 2 (slow)
    thinking

related stimuli, 58

Relevance
    first steps toward, 55–56
    leaking of over time, 87, 98
    reduction of, 150
    Uniqueness and, 97–98

remarkable, being, 56

research
    correct use of, 124
    relevance of, 83–84
    synthesizing data from, 123–124

Resistors, 131–134

resolutions, small, 203

restraining forces, 131–134

reverse benefits, disguised as
    insights, 78

Reverse Claimstorming®, 81–82

reviews, after-action, 88

revisionist history metaphor, 72

risk
    of commission, 88
    of doing nothing, 87–88
    of omission, 87–88
    of status quo, 99

Robinson, Michael, 66

role-playing, 64, 66

Rorschach tests, 114

rules, Confirmation Bias and, 143–144

rules of thumb, 7–8

S

scripts, 111–112

self-censorship, 20

self-doubt, 20

Senge, Peter, 149–150

Shapiro, Stephen, 49

Simon, Herbert, 7

Sivers, Derek, 168

social pressures. *See* Conformity Bias

specific issues, vs. vague unease, 99

split brain, 112–115

stages of innovation. *See* Concept
    Development; Ideation;
    Opportunity Identification
    (Opportunity ID)

statement of purpose, framing,
    167–168

Status Quo Bias, 10, 85–103
    in Concept Development, 96–100
    in Concept Testing, 100–103
    in Ideation, 92–96
    in Opportunity Identification (ID),
        91–92
    risk of status quo, 99
    self-assessment questions, 221–222

steps forward, 189–199

Storz, Beth, 230

streets in Japan example, 168–169

stretch experiences, 51
stretched-beyond-comfort-level ideas,
    118
Sunstein, Cass, 8
surcharge example, 164–165
synthesizing extracted information,
    123–124
System 1 (fast) thinking, 3–5
    cognitive biases and, 4–5, 9
        Confabulation, 107, 110
        Conformity Bias, 126–127
        Negativity Bias, 16, 25, 36–37, 41
    during idea-generation phase, 4
    when beneficial, 6–7
System 2 (slow) thinking, 5–7
    avoidance of, 6
    cognitive biases and
        Confabulation, 110, 112
        Conformity Bias, 126–127
        Negativity Bias, 36–37

T
Takeover exercise, 151–154
Target Areas, 118–119, 181
teamwork, building feeling of, 38–39
Tech Search, 54
temperature of language, 186–187
tension, creative, 149–150
testing of concept. *See* Concept Testing
Thinking, Fast and Slow (Kahneman),
    3, 165
thoughtful laddering in groups, 115
touch typing example, 111–112
Transient Hypofrontality, 114–115
transparent observation, creating
    environment of, 115–117
Trend Hunting, 54

typing example, 111–112

U
umbrella example, 183–184
Uniqueness, 22–24
    first steps toward, 55–56
    lack of, example of, 97–98
    leaking of over time, 98
    reduction of, 150
    Relevance and, 97–98
Unknown Knowns, 52
unrelated stimuli, 58

V
vague unease, vs. specific issues, 99
Vaughn, Christopher, 198
verbatims, 123
visual stimuli, Transient Hypofrontality
    and, 114

W
Wallace, David Foster, 163
Wason, Peter, 144
"Weird, Or Just Different" (Sivers), 168
Westin Hotels example, 161
White Spaces, 181
WISH FOR list, 32–36
Word Salad tool, 172–176
Worlds Excursion, 183–184

Y
"yes, and . . . " vs. "yes, but . . . ," 26–30,
    37–42

Z
Zabelina, Darya, 66
Zandt, Townes Van, 163

About the Authors

Photo by Dan Engongoro,
studio E imaging llc

Adam Hansen, VP Innovation

Adam counts himself fortunate to have enjoyed his entire career in innovation, with the first half of his career spent working on the client side with innovative companies such as Mars and American Harvest, and joining Ideas To Go in 2001.

Adam received his MBA in product management at Indiana University in 1989, where he first saw the potential of a career in innovation while taking Professor Tom Hustad's new product development course. Adam served as VP, Association Development, for the Product Development & Management Association from 2002 to 2004, and volunteers as an innovation strategy expert with select causes and organizations in education and health care.

Outside his work, Adam enjoys his family, music, and the woods surrounding his home in northwestern NJ.

Photo by Andrea Kopacek

Ed Harrington, CEO and Creative Process Advisor

Ed has spent over twenty-five years facilitating ideation and concept development sessions for Fortune 100 companies. He is dedicated to continuously finding impactful ways to uncover insights and generate new ideas for products, services and communications. His particular specialty is in facilitated co-creation sessions where clients collaborate with consumers and customers. Ed believes that, short of the Mona Lisa, anything can be improved.

After receiving his graduate degree from Yale University, Ed cut his teeth as a brand and marketing leader at Proctor & Gamble. He is an Advisory Board Member of the Yale Center for Customer Insights, which gives him exposure to the latest research and methodologies for finding customer insights. Other than pondering new ways to unearth insights and create new ideas, you may also find Ed at his family's cottage in New Hampshire, where he enjoys photography, nature walks, and relaxing, and getting together with one or more of his eight siblings.

Photo by Dan Engongoro,
studio E imaging llc

Beth Storz, President, Innovation Process Facilitator

Giving clients the freedom to explore all the possibilities for their business is one of the reasons Beth Storz loves her job. As president of Ideas To Go, she strives to challenge assumptions and affect change to take clients to the next level, and as a facilitator she helps them bring together all the best ideas to create a great recipe for success. Beth is passionate about recognizing everything people have to offer, then helping them live up to their potential—so, in the end, they can be more innovative.

Beth attended Cornell University where she received a degree in Business Management, and completed her MBA at the New York University Stern School of Business. Beth has nine years of brand management experience at some of the premier consumer packaged goods companies including Unilever, Kraft, and Nabisco. Her experience ranges from managing large flagship brands to smaller strategic portfolios, health and wellness, and innovation. She also has two years of consumer banking experience with Citibank. She attended the Creative Problem Solving Institute for facilitator training, and received focus group moderator training at the RIVA Institute. Outside of work, Beth loves to garden, sing, cook, and crochet, and can readily combine any of the above.